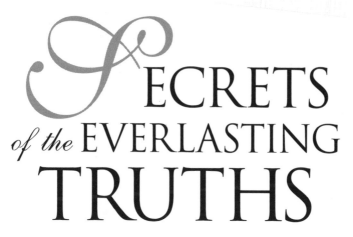

SECRETS of the EVERLASTING TRUTHS

A NEW PARADIGM FOR LIVING ON EARTH

Ryuho Okawa

Happy Science is an imprint of IRH Press Co., Ltd.
IRH PRESS
New York . Tokyo

Library of Congress Control Number: 2012936431
ISBN 13: 978-1-937673-10-9
ISBN 10: 1937673103

Printed in Japan

Cover Image © James Thew-Fotolia.com

Secrets of
The Everlasting Truths

~ A New Paradigm for Living on Earth ~

Ryuho Okawa

Contents

PROLOGUE:
Unearthing the Universe Inside Your Mind

CHAPTER 1:
Becoming a World Religion
~ A Paradigm Shift for Earth People ~

CHAPTER 2:
Faith Will Bring You Miracles

CHAPTER 3:
A New Era of Spirituality

CHAPTER 4:
The Arrival of the New Space Age

CHAPTER 5:
The Time for Salvation Is Here

Foreword by the Publisher

Did you know that miracles are happening around us all the time? In *Secrets of the Everlasting Truths: A New Paradigm for Living on Earth*, Master Ryuho Okawa reveals an extraordinary array of miracles that are increasing in number every day. This book reveals the whys and hows of spiritual phenomena. When you discover these secrets, your view of yourself and the world will be changed dramatically and forever.

Miracles and spiritual occurrences depend not just on Heaven, but ultimately on the *power of our own minds—the power of faith*. Everlasting spiritual laws do exist, and these spiritual laws shape our world and worlds beyond the one we know. It is our knowledge about these laws and our belief in the invisible that will make it possible for us to solve the world's problems and bring our entire planet together. We are on the brink of uniting into one common identity as earth people and creating a brand new era—an era of spirituality. This new era will bring happiness and prosperity to our entire planet for thousands of years to come.

Soon, the mechanisms of spiritual laws will be an intrinsic part of advanced physics, and medicine will no longer be capable of denying that the soul is an essential part of healing. We are also beginning to discover world-changing truths about space people and Earth's deep connection with them. Indeed, our entire planet will experience a decisive paradigm shift regarding the nature of knowledge and truth. This shift will lead to a new era of paradoxical spirituality— in the future, even science will require spiritual knowledge! The solutions to today's problems—environmental, political, scientific, technological, economic, and religious—are *within our own minds.* In these pages, you will discover the spiritual truths that reveal the infinite world of possibilities hidden within your mind. *The door to our future is right within us.*

Preface

Miracles have filled every moment of my life.
I have walked straight forward on my path,
Ever since I discovered how important it is
For today's people
To make each day rich
By discovering the Truths that shine brilliantly
As we find what can only be found
In our dreams and imagination.

It has been my mission to offer spiritual teachings
That will guide people of the present
Throughout their lives.
It has also been my mission
To leave behind valuable messages
For future generations.

I am blazing the trail to a new era of spirituality,
And awakening people to the imminent arrival
Of the new space age.

Through my works,
And in my mind,
I have pictured myself as the modern Buddha,
Who is always prepared to face death
For the sake of the Truths.

The journey of the missionary never ends.
Not a day passes that I do not feel
Powerful winds of the greatest compassion within me,
A compassion that brings rivers of tears to my eyes.
Here, in the following pages, you shall find the laws—
The everlasting Truths.

Ryuho Okawa
Founder and CEO
Happy Science Group
December 2011

PROLOGUE

Unearthing the Universe Inside Your Mind

What Is the Mind?

Through many teachings,
I have explained in great depth valuable perspectives
Regarding life, the world, and many other subjects.
Yet, I hope that you will delve much further
Into the full depth of these teachings:
You must try
To grasp the true meaning of the mind.

Take my teachings,
Including the teachings of the mind,
And try to understand the actual content of the words:
Make them your own,
So that you truly experience them
As your own spiritual enlightenment.

Modern medicine and conventional knowledge

Regard the mind only as a manifestation of brain activity.
But they are mistaken;
Many years of my personal research on the spirit world
Have proven otherwise.
The truth is that the mind
Is not operated by the brain.
In my spiritual research, I have found
That we live on,
Retain our individual ways of thinking,
And continue to produce our individual thoughts,
Even after the human body stops functioning,
Even after it is burned to ashes,
Even after we move on from this life.

The *brain*, therefore, is only *an instrument of the mind*.
The brain is just a channel
That conveys the actions of the mind,
Smoothly, accurately, and quickly.
Thus, when the channel or instrument that is our brain
Ceases to work properly,
The actions of the mind
Simply become imperceptible from outside.

No doubt, many of you will experience
A major paradigm shift in your view of life,

When you discover that we live on
As spiritual beings with everlasting life,
Even after our physical bodies vanish.

Discovering that we retain our thoughts and emotions
Exactly as when we were alive
Might have the impact of the Copernican revolution,
Which definitively changed how we all view the world.

Sometimes, we must follow the example of Columbus,
Who had the revolutionary idea
To sail around the world westward in search of India.
Columbus showed us that there are times
When we must think in unconventional ways.

We must stop studying the physical.
Instead, we must study the soul,
For we can never learn about the mind
By studying only the material.

Only by delving into the soul
And grasping what is there
Can we learn about the workings of the mind.

This means that you will need to change

The way you think,
And the way you have thought
Ever since you can remember.
You need to relearn how to think and perceive.

School and vocational training
Encourage us to establish our ego.
Western thinking teaches us
That the ego is something necessary,
Something we must form,
Something that will be an asset.
It teaches us to draw a clear line
Between ourselves and others
And to take responsibility for our lives.

This idea is not altogether wrong,
But it is only part of the truth.
An education that encourages an ego
Shaped *only* by the material world
Is mistaken.

In shaping our ego,
We should not separate the self and others completely.
Your mind lies deep within your soul,
And is, at its very depths, connected to a much larger world.

Do not separate this larger world from the self.

The World We See Is Just a Drop of Water

Today, we can observe the cosmic universe
Through a telescope,
And we can even explore outer space on a spacecraft.
But we must realize that there is much more to the universe
Than what we can see with our eyes.

If you empty a cup of water on a spacecraft in zero gravity,
It becomes a sphere and floats about.
From the eyes of the Creator of the vast universe,
The Primordial God,
The three-dimensional cosmic universe
Looks like that drop of water floating about in zero gravity.

Now, imagine that inside that drop of water
Live countless invisible microorganisms
Traveling around the universe of that drop of water.
The universe around us,
That our physical eyes perceive,
Is what the microorganisms see
From inside that sphere of water.

We are like those microorganisms.

The Primordial God,
Who exists in a profoundly higher world,
Sees the universe that we see,
Which includes our own gigantic galaxy,
As a tiny drop of water, or a soap bubble
Drifting inside a vastly larger universe.

And in that universe,
Countless similar "soap bubbles"
Are floating about all around.
We can never know just how many
Of these smaller three-dimensional universes exist,
And what the larger world they are a part of is like,
Because it is simply
Beyond the scope of human understanding.

Trying to comprehend this,
Is like the effort of a tiny ant trying to understand
The entire world of human affairs.
So in truth, the world in which we live
Is an enclosed world.
The world outside the microcosm that we see
Is beyond our imagination and impossible to grasp.

How the Universe Began

According to astrophysicists,
The universe began a very long time ago—,
Fifteen billion years ago,
When the Big Bang occurred.
People today believe
That the universe came into being this way,
When a single point in the universe exploded
And began to expand infinitely.

In my book, *The Laws of the Sun*,
I revealed that the Big Bang actually happened
Forty billion years ago.
This is the real truth.

Some have criticized the Big Bang theory,
Saying that it is theoretically impossible:
How could a point in space
Have spontaneously begun to expand infinitely
Fifteen billion years ago,
When neither plane nor location existed?

In answer to this criticism,
Astrophysicists have proposed the inflation theory:

They say that the Big Bang was not the only thing
That created the universe,
But that the universe expanded rapidly in its initial stages;
This rapid expansion created an explosion—the Big Bang—
And then the universe continued to expand.
Other physicists suggest that it was not a linear expansion,
But one that went through fluctuations.

But these theories only avoid the real question
And show that scientists do not yet understand the truth.

From the perspective of Primordial God,
This universe that keeps expanding towards infinity
And progressing through cosmic inflation
Is just a small drop of water.
When He looks into this drop of water,
He sees tiny creatures busily pondering
How their drop of water was created.

We are tiny creatures
Who believe that we possess the ability
To comprehend divine issues
That only God can fathom.
The universe is limitless.
The existence of the universe

Stretches back into an infinite past
And forward into an infinite future.
This is because the universe exists
Inside the Will of Primordial God.
This three-dimensional world materialized into existence
Through the Will and thoughts of Primordial God.

It is because this three-dimensional world was conceived
By Primordial God, the Creator,
That everything within it—
Every sentient creature, every human being—
Carries within itself
A fragment of Primordial God's divine light.

To Find God within You, Love Others

The goal of studying and understanding the mind
Is for us to unearth that fragment of Primordial God—
The fragment of His light
Within us.

There are two ways of unearthing this fragment.
One way is to remove the wall that divides us from others
And to understand that the self and others

Are, in fact, one and the same.
We may perceive many differences between people,
And separate them into me and them,
People from this country and people from that country,
Caucasians, Asians, and blacks,
But we must remember that we are all human.

The diversity we perceive among us
Is just like the divine ray of the great Will,
That passes through a prism
And separates into seven colors.
This is what happens
When the great Will says,
"Humankind, arise."

If we can grasp this truth,
Then *self* and *others* become one,
And our awareness of our oneness with all others
Will manifest in actions that are filled with love.

What is love?
Love is serving others.
Love is giving.
This is unconditional love.

When we practice *giving love*,
We should do more than simply love others
As we love ourselves.
We must try to make the love we provide
Even better and stronger than that:
We must also wish for their growth.

Just as we want to grow into better people ourselves,
We should also want those around us to grow,
And we should want our society to grow and improve.
This kind of love is nurturing love.

We cannot avoid struggles, confrontations,
Differences of opinion,
Complaints, dissatisfactions,
Unfulfilled desires,
And painful attachments,
Because all of us living together on Earth are unique.

But we can surmount all of these struggles
By following the mind of Primordial God.
When we do and break through the wall
That divides us from others,
Forgiveness will arise within us.
This is forgiving love.

And this is why forgiving love is an extremely spiritual love.
We need a magnanimous mind,
One that is deep enough to accept many people,
To surmount the conflicts that occur
Between the ego of one and the ego of another.

We must practice nurturing love,
By showing others the difference between right and wrong,
Correcting injustices,
And encouraging righteousness.
Then, eventually, when we reach a higher state of mind,
We will gain the ability to look beyond right and wrong,
And pursue a world of mutual forgiveness.
This is a spiritual awakening, a spiritual enlightenment.

When we advance even higher,
We realize that as humans born on Earth,
We should become God's hands and feet,
And shine light onto the world
As part of His great light.

When we embody this state of mind,
We become a shining light
That gallops through the world like a graceful breeze,
Illuminating the age we live in.

In this state of mind,
We are not bound by worldly attachments,
But devote our lives completely
To the purpose of radiating light.
I have named this way of life *love incarnate*.

A person who lives this way is light itself.
The presence of this person makes us feel
That God himself, or a part of God,
Is present with us in this age
And living with us on Earth.
This is *love incarnate*.
By thinking of love as a principle of action,
We overcome the barrier between ourselves and others.

Find the Universe in Your Mind

There is another method of studying the mind:
Look into the universe found inside your mind.

Rather than becoming absorbed
In thinking about your human relationships,
About *yourself* in relation to the *world*,
Look into the depths of your own being

And discover the universe inside you.
When we discover that inside,
We are connected to an infinite world,
We reach a state of deep enlightenment.

How do we explore this immeasurable world inside?
First, you must realize
That your education and upbringing thus far
Were only an expedient means
Of helping you make your way through life on Earth.
Now, you must mindfully
Try to shed the shell that is your ego
And enter the inner world within you.
This inner world is what Buddhism calls
The world of egolessness.

It is extremely difficult
To develop egolessness in our daily lives.
That is why the practice of meditation is valuable.

Drop all worldly activities,
Halt the chaos of your thoughts,
And quell the waves of your mind
Until it becomes still like the surface of a tranquil lake,
As you enter into a meditative state—

A boundlessly deep state of egolessness.

A strong ego, one that has become hard like a shell,
Is like a stormy lake with big waves
That seem to have personalities of their own.
A state of egolessness, on the other hand,
Is a peaceful lake
That lies completely still.
All waves have abated completely,
And the surface has become so calm
That the waves are now one with the rest of the lake;
The waves and the lake form a single entity.

Every ripple you find is a part of the ego.
When all waves of the ego subside,
You will enter the infinite world of egolessness
And discover the boundless depths
Inside the calmness of your mind.
There, inside this lake,
Will appear the universe created by God.
In this universe, you will find the path that leads
To the fourth, fifth, sixth,
Seventh, eighth, and ninth dimensions.
This path leads to all of these worlds
And to more paths that lead even further beyond them.

Yet, there is an even higher state.
When you can see the paths to these worlds,
You are still fully aware of the self.
In the next stage of spiritual development,
You will become a part of the universe
And recognize that you help shape the universe.

As we explore the universe inside,
We become aware
That we are one of the building blocks of the universe—
Fragments of light,
Which through God's Will,
Give form to this universe.

We become aware that the same is true for everyone,
And that the same is true for this world on Earth,
And for the fourth, fifth, and sixth dimensions,
And all the higher dimensions
That make up the other world.
The world we go to in our afterlife
Is an expression of God's Will.
You will see that God is light.

Light appears sometimes as particles,
Sometimes as waves.

When light takes the form of particles, matter emerges.
When light takes the form of waves,
It manifests as thoughts, will, or ideas.

When God's Will is concentrated into a single point,
Matter comes into being,
And forms into human beings, planet Earth,
And the three-dimensional universe.
When God's mind
Is *not* concentrated into particles
But appears in the form of electromagnetic waves,
It becomes the spiritual vibrations of thoughts and will
That traverse the universe.
This is the secret of the great universe.

Find Happiness in Oneness With God

The world of spirituality
Reaches far beyond even the most cutting-edge science.
Religion is the science of Truths.
That is why it is valuable to peer into our inner universe,
The world that forms the inside of our mind.

First, follow the principle of love

And overcome the barrier between yourself and others.
Become one with all creatures.

Then, practice egolessness.
Through this Buddhist practice
Of shedding worldly attachments,
You can dive into the depths of your mind,
Wherein lies the mind of God.

This is the moment
When we become one with the universe.
You become the universe,
And the universe becomes you.

If you can reach this state,
You shall savor the most sublime happiness possible—
A lasting happiness
A deep happiness
That will stay with you for a long time to come.

We, human beings, have each incarnated
Hundreds and thousands of times,
With the goal of attaining
This happiness born of enlightenment.

Once you have savored
The sublime happiness called enlightenment,
Material joy will no longer tickle your fancy
And will disappear from you completely.
Even the delight of the heights of worldly glory
Will vanish like spring snow.

Every one of us can achieve happiness
By studying the mind and understanding it.
By becoming aware of the universe inside our minds,
All of us can achieve happiness.

And so I have tried to provide many different teachings,
To show you different angles of this complex Truth.
I am dedicated to unveiling the universe inside your mind.

You shall seek the universe inside your mind.
For there, true happiness awaits you.

Prologue: Unearthing the Universe Inside Your Mind

CHAPTER 1

Becoming a World Religion
~A Paradigm Shift for Earth People~

My Experiences in Brazil

In November 2010, I delivered five lectures during a one-week mission tour to Brazil. The Brazilians who attended my lectures demonstrated a surprisingly high level of spiritual awareness. The depth of their questions and comments about my lectures impressed me.

Although Brazilians live on the opposite side of the globe from Japan, where I mainly lecture, they understand God's Truths, as I teach them, as well or better than Japanese people do. I have published more than eight hundred books in Japanese but only ten in Portuguese[1], the official language of Brazil, as well as some articles that have been translated and published in the Happy Science monthly magazine. This tells me that the Brazilians' understanding of the Truths probably has less to do with the knowledge that they have gained from my books and more to do with the strong faith

---

1. As of December 2011.

intrinsic to Brazilian culture. I felt that their strong foundation of faith raised the overall level of their spirituality.

This was the first time I had spoken to a Brazilian audience. The population of Brazil is 80 percent Catholic, so I was genuinely surprised that they so easily understood the basic teachings of Happy Science. And it wasn't only those who were already members of Happy Science who understood my teachings; the general public understood them as well. Although many of them were hearing me talk for the first time, about 80 percent of the audience who attended my lecture joined Happy Science on the spot. Considering the response in Brazil, I feel that we still have a lot of work to do in Japan.

When I give talks in Japan, a country where materialism, atheism, and left-wing views predominate, the audience tends to be biased against religion and is therefore often resistant to what I say. I often have to start from behind the starting line. I have to combat their prejudices against religion before I can even begin to explain my teachings. I must guide them step by step, so it requires a lot of effort. But when I spoke to an audience of strong faith, I was able to convey my messages much more easily. I found this astonishing.

A Wall of Prejudice against Religion Exists in Japan

A staff member in our International Headquarters once told me that the most difficult countries in which to do missionary work so far are the United States, South Korea, and Japan.

In the case of the United States, part of the difficulty comes from the fact that it is a Christian nation. I also think that Americans feel that their country is culturally superior to other nations, which makes them reluctant to convert to an Asian faith. Still, our membership in the United States has been growing.

In South Korea, I think that the issue is probably related to politics. I understand that people in South Korea harbor negative feelings towards Japan because of the political struggles between the two countries. This situation makes missionary work in Korea an uphill struggle for Happy Science, a religious organization founded in Japan.

As for Japan, it remains one of the most difficult places to spread the Truths, despite my numerous lectures there. It seems as though my messages do not reach Japanese hearts, no matter how many times I speak. It is as difficult as digging a tunnel beneath the ground. So it will take a lot of time to spread the Truths in Japan.

As I mentioned earlier, Japanese people have a strong tendency to disdain or disapprove of religion. When they hear the word *religion*, they automatically respond negatively and immediately want to reject it. Moreover, they believe it is wrong to openly practice or discuss religion. This biased view stands as a wall that blocks them from hearing what we have to say with an open mind. From a political perspective, it is similar to the antireligious wall that exists in North Korea and China. It may not be as thick, but a similar wall endures in Japan, and this wall obstructs the vision of the people and prevents them from seeing clearly.

However, no matter how people feel about religion, only one truth prevails: the spirit world exists. Religions around the world teach that the world of the afterlife, or the spirit world, exists; that God (sometimes called Buddha) and the angels that assist Him in the other world exist; and that the spirit world is largely divided into Heaven and Hell. All major religions of the world share these common ideas. Most world religions also hold that when people leave this world, their destinations in the other world depend on whether they have lived a life that would lead to Heaven or Hell according to the standards of that religion (that is, what each religion considers "right").

In Japan, most people do not believe this. They believe that life is finite and that their existence disappears after a few decades on Earth. This belief persists because of their education and the influence of the mass media.

I have frequently used the word *revolution* to describe the changes that need to take place in Japan. Of course, the revolution I refer to is not an armed revolution, but a spiritual one. We need to bring about a spiritual revolution to establish what is right in Japan and to change Japan to what it should be.

Japan needs to become aware of and prepare to bear its responsibility as the originating country of my teachings of God's Truths. Japan now has the responsibility to become a country that provides and spreads new teachings to the rest of the world. To fulfill this responsibility, Japan needs to raise its level of faith so it can convey my messages to people all around the world. It is urgent that we bring about a spiritual revolution in Japan.

As of December 2011, my teachings have reached more than 90 countries worldwide. It is only a matter of time before it expands to 100, 150, and 200 countries. It may take a few years, but no more than ten. I am sure that people around the world would be shocked to learn that a lack of faith in God is considered normal in Japan. They would find it difficult to believe that Japan is, in fact, a country of such weak religious devotion.

My talks at large lecture halls in Japan are translated and

broadcast worldwide by either live or delayed telecast. Yet, people who listen to the translation of my lectures understand them better than those who listen to them in Japanese. This is a disgraceful situation. It means that the Japanese have acquired knowledge that is totally opposite to the Truths. This wrong knowledge has taken root in the minds of the Japanese people and their society over the course of several decades. Somehow, we have to change this national consensus.

We encounter the same issue in our efforts to change Japanese politics. Japan has plunged into a political crisis. Faced with the threat of attacks from totalitarian military dictatorships in neighboring countries, it has become stricken by paralysis, like a frog being stared down by a snake. However, if the majority of the Japanese people do not believe in God or the afterlife, and instead believe that life ends when they die, then this national consensus bears some resemblance to the perspectives held by North Korea's political leaders and by the members of the ruling Chinese Communist Party in China.

Yes, Happy Science has members in China and North Korea. However, they risk their lives by promulgating their faith. They secretly participate in religious activities despite facing the difficult circumstance of not knowing when or what kind of danger may strike them. Considering the influence that my talks have on Happy Science members and the rest of the world, I feel that it is of paramount importance that I understand the different situations of people in different countries and carefully consider what is right on a global scale, even when I give my teachings in Japan.

The Common Teachings
Among Different Religions

Becoming a world religion may seem like an ambitious challenge for a new religion like us. However, I do not think it is as difficult as it appears.

Conflicts over religious differences occur in countries around the world. This is one of the chief reasons people hate religion. For example, antireligious people point to the conflicts and wars between Christianity and Islam, and quickly assert that religion caused these wars. However, religion itself does not cause these conflicts. Rather, people's misunderstanding of the purpose of religion and their low awareness of religious truths stand at the root of these problems.

At the present moment, differences in laws and political beliefs prevail among countries around the world. But these differences of opinion are specific only to the present day, which is a very brief moment in time compared to the long history of humankind.

All civilizations emerge and perish. New civilizations rise in different countries, but they all become extinct at some point. This pattern repeats around the world. From a larger perspective, the purpose of each new civilization and culture is to guide people to move toward happiness. There were many experimental factors in the past civilizations, but still, humans have learned through trial and error and accumulated a rich variety of experiences. So, I do not want the human race's past efforts to be in vain.

Different kinds of civilizations and various types of religions have existed, but it would not be right to simply focus on their differences. Instead, I would like you to look for the same Golden Road that runs through all of them and become aware of the existence and the teachings of the supreme being who is trying to guide people on a global scale.

What, then, are the common teachings that you can find in every civilization and religion? What teachings come from the supreme being that guides people on a global scale? The first one, I believe, is the teaching of love. Upon hearing the word love, many people probably think of love between a man and a woman or heterosexual love. However, this understanding of love is not enough.

Jesus taught love for God and love for our neighbors.

When asked what the most important lesson in the world was, Jesus replied: "You shall love the Lord your God with all your heart, and with all your soul, and with all your mind. This is the greatest and first commandment. And a second is like it: you shall love your neighbor as yourself" (Matt. 22:37–39). Jesus preached forms of love beyond heterosexual love and the love for those close to us, but I think this is still not enough. I believe that one more important form of love exists.

What is this important form of love? Apart from the love of simply being kind to others, we need to practice love that guides people to the right path. If you truly love others, whether they are your neighbors, strangers, or those close to you, you need to urge them to enter the right path. I have lectured on the teachings of love numerous times. But I want to emphasize that guiding those you meet in life to the right path is also a form of love. Love includes guiding people to Right Faith. Please remember this.

I also would like you to know, even though it may be difficult for some people to understand this concept, that to love the lord God is to become one with Him, and that loving the lord God is the same as loving yourself.

An Important Task for Religious Leaders

To enter the right path, you need to live with the perspective that the other world exists. For many people, whether the next world exists or doesn't exist may appear to be a toss-up. They can never be sure what awaits them after they die.

But in fact, I have provided a great deal of evidence of the existence of a spirit world. In 2010 alone, I published fifty-one books, many of them based on the publicly recorded spiritual messages I received from more than 160 spirits. In this way, I have provided substantial proof to the public that even after people die and return to Heaven, they retain the personalities they had when they were alive and try to guide the people of this world from the spirit world.

Everybody is free to believe this or not. But at the very least, I think that no one in this world would be able to instantly switch between the personalities of more than 160 people and convey their different messages.

I can provide as much proof as you would like of the existence of another world—the world of the afterlife. I continue to provide proof today and can keep proving it from now on, if necessary. However, no one has ever proven that the other world or the afterworld does not exist. No one has ever proven that humans do not possess souls, either.

Many people have expressed the opinion that the other world and souls do not exist. But really, they are just declaring their lack of belief and faith on a personal level. By doing so, however, they spread the virus of disbelief, leading people astray from the path of faith.

On the last day of their lives, people may realize the existence of the spirit world. But that is not enough. Because I see angels and their supporting spirits trying earnestly to help those who returned to a world of suffering, I feel compelled to tell people in this world that they still have a lot of work to do. We do not want our contemporaries to return to a world of suffering in the future.

Never forget that many people are seriously and earnestly trying to assert the existence of the other world. Indeed, this has been one of the most important tasks for religious leaders throughout history.

Now is the time for today's religious leaders to reawaken to their purpose and fulfill their mission. As long as we live in this material world, it is difficult to believe in the existence of the invisible spirit world, let alone convince others to believe in it. Yet, religious leaders must strive to accomplish this difficult task.

A society and its people should respect their religious leaders. Unfortunately, in Japan, public education and mass media propaganda have repeatedly planted negative images of religious leaders in people's minds. It is the mission of Happy Science to tear down this antireligious wall.

Ever since I attained my great enlightenment about thirty years ago, I have been consistently working hard to carry out my mission. However, now I have an ever-increasing feeling that I have yet to fulfill my original purpose.

My earnest desire to convey God's Truths to people all over the world has underscored for me the necessity of first bringing fundamental change to my home country of Japan. Japan needs to once again become a nation with a high level of spirituality and awareness of the Truths.

Our basic doctrine of the Fourfold Path consists of the principles of Love, Wisdom, Self-Reflection, and Progress. Missionary work has always been part of the teaching of Progress; however, our missionary work is not only about activities that develop our organization or increase our membership. When you guide people onto the right path, you save them and their souls, and you help them make the most of their lives while here on Earth.

Faith Will Lead to Salvation

Jesus taught that the most important doctrine is: "You shall love the Lord your God with all your heart, and with all your soul, and with all your mind"(Matt. 22:37). Some people may feel that this teaching has nothing to do with them.

To those people I say: I am fully aware that it may be difficult for you to believe me when I say that I, a person who was born in this modern age, once guided Buddha, Jesus, and Mohammed from Heaven to help them establish Buddhism, Christianity, and Islam—all world religions that today have hundreds of millions of believers. However, facts are facts and the truth is the truth. My consciousness resides in Heaven, as a supreme being called El Cantare, who not only sent the founders of Buddhism, Christianity, and Islam to Earth, but also guided them while they were on Earth. El Cantare, who led the creation of these world religions, has now been born in Japan, and he is committed to fulfilling his ultimate responsibility.

I have been working to spread these teachings in this world for nearly thirty years, and I still have a little more time before the end of my service. Until then, will I be able to enlighten the world through my teachings? Or will skeptics destroy or conceal my teachings forever? A battle that will determine our future is about to begin on a global scale. The Last Judgment for humankind is whether people around the world believe my teachings. That is the question I am posing to the human race now.

My teachings are not only for people today, not only for

our current lifetime, and not only for this era. Those who are alive now will eventually leave this world. My teachings are also designed for future generations of people, in different parts of the world, who somehow manage to survive. We need to pass down these teachings to future generations.

Buddhism, Christianity, and Islam are teachings of the past, and will not be able to provide guidance for people who will be living in the future from the twenty-first century to the thirtieth and fortieth centuries. Now is the time to disseminate new teachings that will guide humankind through the years to come.

The future will be built upon my teachings. Future civilizations will be built upon my words. Even if all is lost, humans will have hope as long as my words remain. In Greek mythology, Pandora opened the box and released all the evils of the world. Only one item remained in the box—hope. My words are the hope in Pandora's Box. The future of humankind will be surely built upon my words.

I request that all those who believe in my teachings attempt to guide others to enter the right path. More importantly, our ultimate goal is to pass these teachings down from generation to generation, and convey them all over the world against all odds. If my teachings of the Truths reach all corners of the world, they will certainly ignite people's hearts, and these people also will spread the Truths. It doesn't matter where it starts. It could be Japan that will start the worldwide movement of salvation, but it does not need to be. It could be any country in the world.

In fact, membership in India is growing rapidly and is catching up with membership in Japan. In the next few years, membership in India will probably surpass that of Japan. People in India have already accepted the fact that I am the reincarnation of Shakyamuni Buddha, but the Japanese are still doubtful.

Buddha was the only person who has ever been able to leave all his teachings as religious scriptures, and the only person who would be able to do this today would be Buddha. The laws of the Truths that I preach also will be compiled and remain as sacred scriptures. I have taught the Truths in Japan for more than twenty years and have delivered more than 1,600 lectures[2] that have been published as books.

In 2010 alone, I published fifty-one books that were sold in bookstores. I also published eleven books available exclusively to Happy Science members. It's not possible for a single person living on Earth to achieve this. The spirits in Heaven have gathered all their powers at this time to send their messages to people on Earth.

---

2. As of December 2011.

I am now sending a wake-up call to unawakened governments, the unawakened business world, the unawakened cultures, and the unawakened academic world. I continue to impart my message that they need to open their eyes and awaken to the Truths.

As members of Happy Science engaging in missionary work, you may face a thick wall obstructing your activities to spread your faith. Some people may rebuff or ridicule you. However, you should not let them daunt you. There is nothing to fear, because El Cantare and his many Divine Spirits in Heaven are by your side and support you.

In the past, I have repeatedly preached that we can only take our mind with us when we return to the other world. But in recent years, I have boldly declared that the only thing we should take with us to the other world is Right Faith.

In Buddhism, Right Faith means practicing Right View, the first principle in the Eightfold Path that Shakyamuni Buddha taught. You can practice Right View only when you see things based on Right Faith. If we do not have Right Faith, we will see the world in an entirely different light. Our perspectives of what is right and wrong will be reversed, and we will begin to see acts of love for others as evil acts, and see evil acts as good. To practice Right View is to have Right Faith. Only when you have Right Faith can you see and observe things rightly.

Awaken as Earth People

As I mentioned, I have been providing proof for the existence of the spirit world for many years. Therefore, people around the world are gradually beginning to accept and absorb the Truths I have been teaching. Although it is taking a long time for people in Japan to assimilate my teachings, people in countries where I have never traveled are already beginning to embrace them.

Many highly educated and intellectual people in Japan ridicule or look down on people who believe in the spirit world. These people often feel the same way about those who believe in extraterrestrials.

If we look at the night sky, we see numerous stars. An infinite number of galaxies exist that are about the same size as our galaxy. It is impossible to count the number of galaxies that populate the great universe. Given these infinite numbers of galaxies, it is absurd to presume that humanlike or intelligent beings only exist on our planet. In fact, this is an incredibly arrogant idea. Simply put, it is a mistake to think that among the zillions of stars in the universe, humankind exists only on planet Earth. The refusal to accept the existence of extraterrestrials constitutes a kind of faith, but I have to say, it is an absurd faith and one that is in error.

Some stars are inhabited by beings with a highly developed intellect similar to that of humankind on Earth. Inhabitants of other stars have developed civilizations far more advanced than ours. They would not be able to travel across time and space from the faraway universe and come to Earth unless their civilizations were much more developed than ours. Many of them are here on Earth now. In fact, more than twenty species of extraterrestrials have come to Earth. Now they are waiting for Earth to enter the new space age.

Humans on Earth have developed and launched space rockets and are gradually making their way into space. Soon, humans will begin to interact with extraterrestrials on an equal footing. Space people are waiting expectantly for that moment.

One of my missions is to help develop humankind to the cultural level necessary to communicate with these beings from outer space. As I look at the current situation from outside Japan, I am very saddened by the fact that my teachings of the Truths haven't disseminated widely enough in Japan, where my teachings originate.

People today will have difficulty accepting my teachings about the universe and space people. But this does not change the fact that many extraterrestrials are already here on Earth and that other extraterrestrials infiltrated Earth during past civilizations and have become naturalized as earth people. I have been revealing these facts since 2010, and I will continue to bring these facts to light in an effort to help people understand and accept them more easily. By teaching the laws of the universe, I am trying to build the foundation for humans to communicate and culturally interact with beings from outer space.

Proving the existence of the other world alone is hard enough. But I am now notifying people that we will start interacting with our space brothers and sisters soon. The new space age is drawing near. Announcing this shocking fact requires a lot of courage. However, we must overcome this difficulty. I earnestly wish, with all my heart, that my messages will prevail throughout the world and be passed down to future generations so that people in the future will be able to use them as guidance to survive any catastrophic situation.

Human beings on Earth are not small beings living alone on a small planet in the universe, and numerous other beings in the universe have faith in God. Space people will eventually reveal themselves and try to interact with us humans on Earth. I am providing these teachings to help you prepare for that moment.

Some readers may make a mockery of my words, but

before you do, please try to open your heart and listen to my words with an open mind. I am giving you teachings you probably have not learned before. You just do not know the facts. Please do not judge right and wrong about something you do not know. Please stop judging the Truths. Instead, please accept the unknown. I ask you to believe that the future will open from the unknown.

This is the message I would like to impart in this chapter titled "Becoming a World Religion," and this is what I mean by "a paradigm shift for earth people." I am calling for a fundamental change in the mindset of people on Earth.

Let us awaken as *earth people* and rise up for the future of humanity. I hope we can all work on this together.

CHAPTER 2

Faith Will Bring You Miracles

Many Miracles Are Occurring Now

Miracles of healing are not unusual at Happy Science, and there have been more of them lately because the faith of my followers is gaining in strength. I said in the past that if the faith of my followers were to grow stronger, miracles would increase by a hundredfold. Sure enough, the number of miracles is rising. While traveling in India and Nepal in February and March 2011, I gave four lectures in English. In Bodhgaya, India, an audience member had not been able to use his hand for many years because of muscle atrophy. As he was listening to my lecture, he suddenly regained the ability to move his hand. It was a miracle. I didn't have an intention to cure any illnesses through my lecture, but this miracle occurred while I was speaking. This person is now living testimony that miracles do occur. Another miracle took place on April 17, 2011, at the Happy Science temple in Kokura, in Fukuoka Prefecture, Japan, when I gave the lecture that later formed the content of this chapter. In the afternoon on the day before my lecture, one of the members of our temple was rushed to the hospital after developing symptoms of brain hemorrhage. He teetered on the verge of death, but happily, the prayer services that our members held for him intervened to save his life. He left the hospital that same day. This miracle was the fruit of this person's strong faith.

I could mention many other cases; this type of healing miracle has accelerated in recent days. Many miracles occurred during the Japanese earthquake of 2011. In its wake, the earthquake and tsunami left approximately sixteen thousand dead and four thousand missing, according to a November 2011 report by the National Police Agency. From early reports, I was notified that two of our members had died and two more were missing. (In the final count, eight of our members died.) To my surprise, those who had died or were missing were members who had joined Happy Science on the recommendation of their families but had continued to oppose Happy Science. It is frightening to see how in one family, those who wholeheartedly took part in our activities survived while those who were opposed died.

It was a relief to find that we lost very few members in this great earthquake. Considering the magnitude of the disaster, I anticipated a possible loss of more than a thousand followers. It is truly a miracle that the number of our members who actually perished through this disaster was significantly smaller than that.

Moreover, all Happy Science buildings remained in working condition even after the earthquake. The tsunami flooded only one venue, which was a rented space for one of our temples. Thanks to the care and efforts of my followers who helped restore the building, on March 23, ten days after the disaster hit, the members of this temple were able to hold there the Great Enlightenment Celebration, a yearly event to commemorate my great enlightenment. This was quite unbelievable.

I have said before that if a town had only a hundred people living in it who believed in me, catastrophic natural disasters would not affect that area. In fact, 130 of our believers lived in a part of the Tohoku where the disaster struck hard. The area found itself miraculously spared, even though the tsunami brought destruction to the surrounding regions. In other cases, the tsunami swept away nearby houses but left our believers' homes untouched, while the disaster completely devastated regions where none of our members lived.

Many followers experienced other types of mysterious phenomena at the time, such as the tsunami suddenly pulling back in the opposite direction, or waves passing very close to their houses, but not flowing in. One member gave us this testimony: "Just as I was escaping in my car, I suddenly got an inspiration that said to abandon the car. So I got out and climbed up the dikes. I found a railroad track where a train had stopped due to the earthquake. The conductor told me to jump on, so I did. Soon after, the tsunami came. The railroad tracks immediately near the train vanished, but the train itself was left untouched."

I heard so many similar testimonies that I could not help but express my amazement. Believers' testimonies of such miracles inspire me tremendously and instill me with great energy.

Miracles Are Found Throughout Recorded History

Water-Related Miracles: Jesus Christ and Shakyamuni Buddha

These amazing stories are actually not uncommon when you review the past. Many miracles have occurred throughout history, especially water miracles. For example, the Bible tells a story of Jesus walking on the waters of a lake. The Bible also recounts how Jesus calmed the stormy waves of a lake by shouting at it. That story describes how Jesus and his disciples were sailing on a lake when they got caught in a storm. Heavy winds and huge waves were about to overturn the boat. The disciples were petrified. But when Jesus shouted to the wind and waves, the storm abated quickly and the lake became calm once again, surprising his disciples. From stories like this one, we know that it is possible to quell waves.

A particularly common type of water miracle, found often in history, is the phenomenon of water pulling back. In the famous Exodus story, the waters of the Red Sea parted for Moses. Most people today probably have difficulty believing this account. The Red Sea today is very deep, so it was likely a different body of water, probably what is now a swamp area a little further north. In fact, a phenomenon occurs there whereby the easterly winds blow so fiercely that it splits the waters. This phenomenon must have occurred when Moses prayed.

Likewise, towards the end of the movie *The Chronicles of Narnia: The Voyage of the Dawn Treader*, a scene shows the waters of the beach pulling back to form a wall, and King Aslan, in the form of a lion, walking alongside it. As you can see, this "pulling back of water" is a well-known occurrence. In Buddhist texts, legends also exist about Shakyamuni Buddha flying over a river, and Buddha parting the water of the Ganges River at one of its wider points so he could walk across a dry riverbed to the other side.

The many water-related miracles in the Bible and in Buddhist scriptures demonstrate that miracles involving water do occur. We therefore can say that the testimonies from the Japanese earthquake of 2011 that tell of water pulling back in the opposite direction and water not entering certain houses are certainly plausible. If a tsunami threatens one of our temples in the future, you should recite our prayer, 'El Cantare, fight!' in a version such as 'Prayer for wave-splitting! El Cantare, fight!' This recitation can split waves since the waves will have an aversion to the prayer and so will be more likely to avoid you.

Miracles That Saved Famous Disciples from Executions

Many other kinds of miracles have been recorded in historical documents. The Kannon Sutra, which is part of the Buddhist Lotus Sutra, contains a section for protecting people from the threat of fire and the threat of water, or, in other words, protecting people from disasters involving fire and water. This means that one of the blessings of the Lotus Sutra is protection from death by fire or flood.

The Kannon Sutra also mentions another type of miracle, one that saves people from being slain by a sword. It says that the sword will break before it touches the victim, thus sparing them. Nichiren, a famous Japanese Buddhist monk of the thirteenth century, cites his own experience of this miracle. Nichiren, an adherent of the Lotus Sutra, was about to be executed at the Tatsunokuchi execution ground. According to records from that period, when the executioner raised the sword to strike, a shiny object flew from the region of Enoshima Island towards the city of Kamakura. As it was an unidentified object, it could have been a UFO. But the records describe a shiny object like the moon flying through the sky from Enoshima towards Kamakura. "At that moment," say the records, "the sword shattered into pieces," saving Nichiren's life.

Since Nichiren wrote this description himself, it is probable that he used the phrase, "shattering of the sword," which appears in the Kannon Sutra, as a metaphor to describe what happened to him on the execution ground. However, Nichiren was, in fact, due to be executed, so we can assume that some kind of miracle must have saved him.

The story continues, saying that the executioner was at a loss and wondering what to do when a messenger from the government arrived and told him, "Wait! Don't kill him. We could be cursed for killing a priest. We will change his sentence to exile to the land of Sado." Thus, the words of the Kannon Sutra—"being saved even when about to be slain by a sword"—had actually come true and saved Nichiren's life.

The Bible recounts other similar miracles, including some related to imprisonment for execution. After Jesus died, authorities arrested and imprisoned his disciples. The scripture describes several miracles in which prison doors opened and set the disciples free. In one case, an angel guided the jailed Peter to the iron gate of the city, which opened on its own (Acts 12:6-10; Acts 5:19-20 and Acts 16:26-28 describe similar miracles). From these sacred texts, we can see that miracles were a common occurrence during particular periods of history.

Resurrection Miracles: Osiris and Jesus Christ

Most of you are probably familiar with these two famous resurrection miracles. The first one is about the resurrection of the famous Egyptian god Osiris, who was known in Greece as Ophealis. Osiris, a ninth-dimensional spirit and one of the brother souls of El Cantare, was born in Greece more than six thousand years ago. As king, he ruled Egypt, which was a dominion of Greece at the time. The Egyptian goddess Isis was his wife.

I mentioned earlier that the life of a member of the Happy Science temple in Kokura was saved on April 16, 2011, just as I was recording a spiritual message in my hotel room. As preparation for the lecture I was planning to give the next day, titled "The Spirit World and Miracles," I summoned Edgar Cayce as a guiding spirit to assist me in conducting a spiritual reading to investigate how Osiris was resurrected from death.

Osiris's death was plotted by his own brother, Set. Osiris was often away from the palace on foreign expeditions, and in his absence, his younger brother Set had usurped the throne. Later, when Osiris returned from abroad, Set plotted to kill his brother during a banquet held to lure Osiris into a deadly trap. As part of the entertainment, Set had prepared a coffin and invited people to step inside. "The one who fits perfectly will be presented with this coffin," he said. Many tried, but no one fit perfectly. When Osiris's turn came, he fit perfectly inside this coffin designed specifically for him. Then, as soon as Osiris lay down into the coffin, its lid was shut and nailed tight, trapping him inside.

They made it impossible for Osiris to escape and threw the coffin into the Nile River. The coffin apparently floated out to the sea, all the way to the coast of what is present-day Syria. When Isis heard about the incident, she immediately went in search of the coffin. Then, through the efforts of the queen and her entourage, the cold body of Osiris was miraculously brought back to life.

However, the evil King Set could not stand for Osiris to continue living. So he captured him again and killed him a second time, this time cutting his body into pieces and burying them in different places. Set was sure that now, no one would be able to bring Osiris back to life ever again. It was nothing short of a mutilation murder.

However, Isis and her maids and servants brought him back to life a second time. They searched out all the dismembered parts of his body, reassembled them, and wrapped his body in bandages. (By the way, this healing process became the beginning of the famous mummification practices.) Then, Isis and the others prayed fervently.

From here on, this story includes information that I gathered through my space-people readings. At the time that Osiris and Isis lived, space people were visiting Earth from the star Vega, and these space people possessed special healing power. Some of the Vegans helped Isis resurrect Osiris with a healing method called Vega Healing. Thanks to the help of the Vegans, Osiris was resurrected as an almighty god with superhuman abilities.

At Happy Science, we offer a ritual prayer service for healing illnesses called "Super Vega Healing." It was this very prayer that my members said for the follower who was on the verge of death with a subarachnoid hemorrhage. It helped save his life.

Though this insight only appeared once throughout my space-people readings, and requires further investigation to confirm it, one of my space-people readings revealed that the inhabitants of Vega also played a role in the resurrection of Jesus. Jesus died on the cross on a Friday afternoon; he drew his last breath around three o'clock in the afternoon. While on the cross, Jesus was stabbed in the ribs with a spear, draining him of the blood in his body; he was then buried in a cave. Three days later on a Monday morning, he was resurrected to life.

A large rock had covered the entrance where Jesus's body had been placed. However, when Mary Magdalene and several other women went to see his grave on that Monday morning, to their astonishment they found the entrance open and the body of Jesus gone. "Somebody has taken away the body of our Lord!" they lamented. At that moment, an angel dressed in white descended and asked the women what was wrong. Mary replied, "Someone has taken away the body of our Lord." As Mary turned around, to her utter surprise, she saw Jesus standing before her.

"Nonsense!" you may think. However, it is a fact that the resurrection of Jesus was an integral part of the formation of Christianity. At the age of thirty, Jesus began preaching and spreading his teachings, and soon after at the age of thirty-three, he was crucified and executed with two criminals. At the time of Jesus's arrest and crucifixion, Jesus's group of disciples had literally disassembled, and only two or three female disciples and John and several other male disciples were present with him. If the story had completely ended there, Christianity would never have grown into a world religion. There were others like him who had been arrested and executed for carrying out religious activities, but their respective religious movements ended completely with their death. Christianity has lasted because Jesus Christ's resurrection gave his followers strength, and helped them to rapidly transform into a missionary order.

Since the Bible states that more than five hundred people saw Jesus's resurrection, I do not doubt that it is true. If more than five hundred witnesses attest that they saw him, it is too large a number to justify dismissing it as a false account. All of his leading disciples, including the most skeptical of them, Saint Thomas, as well as many other people, witnessed the resurrection of Jesus. (The Gospel of Thomas was not included in the official Bible, although he was one of the twelve apostles. But the document exists.)

John 20:24–29 describes the account of the interaction between the resurrected Jesus and Saint Thomas. It says that when Jesus's disciples gathered to tell Thomas that Jesus has arisen, Thomas said: "Unless I see the mark of the nails in his hands, and put my finger in the mark of the nails and my hand in his side, I will not believe." Several days later, when the disciples had gathered again in a room with all the doors locked, Jesus entered without opening the door, much like a ghost. Jesus said to Thomas, "Thomas, is this what you want to see?" Jesus showed him his hands with the scars from the nails. Thomas, surprised, shouted to Jesus, "My Lord!" Later on, Jesus said to Saint Thomas, "It is a shame that you have to see proof to believe. True faith is to believe without seeing."

Thus, the Bible tells us that Jesus visited many people after his resurrection. I used to think that it was his spirit that everyone saw, but this doesn't seem to be the case every time. Of all the Christian ideologies, there was one in particular that I could not understand for years, and this was the idea of the "rapture," in which one's body rises into the air. I always wondered how this phenomenon could be explained, because it is usually the spirit that ascends; the body cannot be raised into the air. However, the New Testament clearly says that upon the return of Jesus in the future, many people will be raised into the air.

After I began to conduct space-people readings, however, I learned a lot and realized that only one thing could explain this phenomenon: light beams from UFOs. The light beam of a UFO can lift a person off the ground. I realized that this would explain how a body could rise into the air, and I also realized that this has actually happened.

I once did a reading on a man whose subconscious revealed that he had been a Vegan in the past and that he had been with other Vegans on their spaceship when Jesus was executed. He said, "We pulled Jesus into the spaceship, healed him, and resurrected him." In a series of space-people readings, this story was only mentioned once, so I would like to verify it from different perspectives. But if it turns out to be true, it would prove that it is possible for someone to rise physically into the air. Vegans are a thousand years ahead of Earth scientifically and technologically, which explains why it is possible for them to cure many illnesses.

Even after two thousand years, more than two billion people on Earth still believe the story of the Bible, of a man who died on a cross, whose death was confirmed with the stab of a spear, who was put in a tomb, and who nonetheless resurrected physically. If the resurrection of Jesus was a lie, it would not have endured and had such historical impact. This was possible because the conviction of the people who witnessed these events was absolute.

Faith Is the Key to Unlocking Miracles

Many unbelievable things will occur in this world from now on. Previously unthinkable phenomena will take place. For example, we may encounter space people who try to show us their scientific and technological superiority, or people may experience a spiritual power giving them assistance. As the history of Happy Science grows longer, many miracles will continue to occur, and we will document them, creating a record much like the Bible and Buddhist scriptures.

The key to this is faith. Faith really makes miracles possible. In most cases, it depends completely on whether we do or do not have the strength to believe. When we do not believe, it means that we are perceiving situations based on the rules of the material world. If we allow our ways of thinking and perceiving to be at the mercy of the rationalizations of the physical world only, nothing out of the ordinary will ever happen.

On the other hand, when we have faith and believe, then we do not succumb to the rules of this world. We accept the existence of a power that lies beyond this world and comes to us from higher worlds that exist in different dimensions from ours. When we accept this fact, various phenomena are given a chance to occur.

For example, a follower told us a story about a motorcycle accident. "One day, I was riding my motorbike, and I collided with a car. I was thrown into the air, and there was no time to recite the entire prayer. So in my mind, I drew the sign of the cross and the sign of the star of 'El Cantare, Fight.' When I hit the ground, I was left completely unscathed while my bike was completely wrecked." His faith in El Cantare saved his life.

This person was in the air for just a few seconds. However, from the perspective of other dimensions, time is something that can be frozen. Even in the short interval of an instant, many things can occur. The range of things that can happen is endless.

Fire-Related Miracles:
The Stories of Two Japanese Gods

Just as secret techniques to reversing waves and parting water exist, so do secret techniques for miraculously reversing the approach of fire. In Japanese history, Yamato Takeru, a legendary Japanese prince, was someone who did this. Yamato Takeru undertook an expedition to bring peace and order to all territories of Japan. While he was in present-day Yaizu, in Shizuoka Prefecture, his enemies attacked him with fire. The fields around Yamato Takeru were set ablaze, and the fire spread and surrounded him very quickly. So he drew the sword of Kusanagi and slashed the grass around him, as some type of spiritual rite.

These efforts alone could not have stopped the fire; nonetheless, the fire completely changed direction and instead advanced on his enemies. Takeru not only escaped a close call with death, but also killed his enemies in their own fire. This shows us that if a fire approaches us, we can miraculously send it in the opposite direction.

Ōkuninushi also escaped fire. His story is mixed with myths and legends and contains some confusing elements, but basically, accounts say that Ōkuninushi's brothers were very jealous of him. They were spiteful towards him and treated him with great malice. One day, they set fire to the fields near him. He was about to be burned alive when suddenly, a mouse appeared and told him, "Outside, there is very little room. Inside, it is hollow. Dig here." When Ōkuninushi checked underground, it was indeed hollow, and he survived by waiting in the underground cavity until the fire passed. As we can see, spiritual techniques—spiritual laws of the universe—do allow people to escape fire attacks.

Other Miracles in Christianity and Buddhism

So far, I have mentioned miracles that involved escaping the dangers of fire and water, resurrecting the dead, and escaping the strike of a sword by shattering the blade. Other recollections of miracles involve escaping from confinement, even with shackled hands and feet and locked doors. The Bible cites a couple of examples.

The first occurred to Peter, the first pope in the history of Christianity. Peter was the disciple who denied Jesus three times before the cock crowed twice to avoid arrest. He eventually reclaimed his allegiance to Jesus, but while he was doing missionary work in Rome, authorities took him into custody. In Acts 12:6–11, soldiers threw Peter into prison and bound him in chains. Suddenly, an angel appeared in the cell. Peter's chains fell away, and he fled. He experienced a miracle of escaping from a prison despite his shackled hands and feet. Later, Peter would eventually become a martyr in Rome.

Another miracle occurred to Paul, one of Christianity's most famous early missionaries, although he is not one of the twelve apostles. Paul was a keen student of Judaism, which existed before Christianity, and thought that Christianity was a deceptive religion. He persecuted the Christians. Armed with a warrant, he went around arresting Jesus's disciples.

Acts 9:3–19 tells how one day, on the road to Damascus, Paul's life took a complete turn. While chasing after Christians, Paul (who was still named Saul at this time) encountered a dazzling light from the sky that completely blinded him for about three days. Later, Ananias, one of the Christians that Paul was chasing and trying to arrest that day, visited him. Ananias put his hand on Paul and healed his eyes. In that moment, Paul experienced the love of the Christians and converted to Christianity. After his sight was restored,

Paul, the man who had made it his mission to arrest Christians, experienced a complete transformation and became a Christian missionary himself.

Jesus had performed a similar healing miracle; after Jesus prayed in the Garden of Gethsemane, some people came to arrest him. In an effort to protect Jesus, Peter drew his sword and cut off one of their ears. Jesus then put his hand on the injured man's ear and healed it.

Both stories teach us to love our enemies, and show why Christianity has spread so far and wide. As you can see, religious history is filled with many miracles. This is very important for everyone to remember.

In comparison with other religions, Buddhism tends not to emphasize the occurrence of miracles. But if we read the Buddhist scriptures carefully, we will find many accounts of miracles. For example, the Three Pure Land Sutras tell the story of Queen Vaidehi. Her son, an evil king, captured her and locked her in prison. The Buddha and his disciples then flew through the sky and appeared in the prison to console her with his teachings. From the description, it seems that their spirits entered the prison by leaving their bodies.

Buddhism today downplays these miracles; for instance, the influential Buddhist scholar Hajime Nakamura was a rationalist who did not believe these stories and had difficulty understanding them. Today's religious scholars try to stay away from these questions. Nevertheless, there are many stories about Buddha floating in the air and giving sermons while hovering.

Faith Will Protect You from Disasters

When a miracle happens, the forces of other dimensions are at work in various ways. As Happy Science expands worldwide, many incredible miracles in a variety of forms will occur. I do not know who will be the beneficiaries of those miracles, but of one thing I am sure: those in our temples with strong faith will be the ones to make them happen. The faith of my followers will overpower the physical laws of the material world. We can make more and more miracles happen.

People may ask me, "So, why couldn't you stop the tsunami and the Great East Japan Earthquake?" Some people might even try to mock us. But dear friends, we still need more believers. The Great East Japan Earthquake was undoubtedly a warning from Heaven. And, at the same time, a force protected the faithful ones. However, we still do not have enough followers of faith. As I mentioned earlier, if as few as one hundred of our believers live in a town, catastrophic natural disasters will not strike there. But we do not have more than a hundred believers in every single town. In some places, we have no followers at all, or only a scattering.

Moreover, there are many skeptics that just can't be saved. Even if they were saved, they would not understand what happened to them. They would write it off as only a physical or natural phenomenon. Bending the laws of nature will be meaningless unless they can see that the presence of more believers makes more miracles possible.

Does it seem like a carrot and stick approach? Well, that is one way of seeing God's intentions. When progress, prosperity, and pleasure are achieved in times when the prevalence of faith and spirituality has declined, people tend to forget God's Truths. However, if God only meted out punishment to show them their error, then people would fear Him, making it even more difficult for them to believe in Him. That is why he provides a mixture of events, ones that frighten us and miracles that give us hope.

The calamitous scope of the Japanese earthquake of 2011 could well be a sign of imminent major earthquakes in other places. Other types of disasters, such as tsunamis and volcanic eruptions, are also possible. Nevertheless, please remember that the histories of the world religions are sprinkled with many miracles. Moses parted the waters of the Red Sea, and Jesus shouted at the waves on the lake to calm the storm. And the one who guided Moses and Jesus was no one but me. Therefore, if my believers have genuine faith in me, I assure you that many miracles will occur, and someday, they will be written down in the next "Bible." I invite you to become a living witness of our miracles.

A Successful Exorcism in *The Rite*

In this chapter, "Faith Will Bring You Miracles," we have studied many examples of miracles. Faith was the main factor in all of them. We can take this topic of faith further: faith can also intervene in personal catastrophes. Possession by evil spirits causes 70 or 80 percent of illnesses. In cases of very serious illnesses, it is especially possible that the ailing person is very close to being possessed by the devil. However, as long as the ill can find faith, they can be healed and saved.

In 2011, the film *The Rite* was released. This film was almost like a sequel to the movie *The Exorcist*. It depicted the training of exorcists that, in fact, is the actual training conducted in the Vatican, or the Holy See, the central government of the Catholic Church. The Vatican aims to send at least one exorcist to each of its dioceses in Italy.

Fourteen exorcists live in the United States, and *The Rite* chronicles the real experience of an exorcist in the diocese of

Chicago. I recommend that my followers watch this movie. Anthony Hopkins is the lead actor in this film—so you can expect it to be quite frightening—and he plays a man who has performed over two thousand exorcisms. This character becomes discouraged after someone he was trying to help dies. Taking advantage of his doubt, the devil possesses him.

The demon that entered the body identified itself as Baal. Baal is also known as Belial, but it is essentially referring to Beelzebub. It is the same demon that tempted Jesus in the wilderness and challenged him to transform stones into bread and to jump off a cliff.

At this point in the movie, a young theology student intervenes. This student is the future exorcist of the Chicago Diocese, and he is still inexperienced. He is also not fully convinced that the devil exists, but eventually, he opens his heart to faith and begins his battle with the devil.

When the devil asks the young exorcist, "Do you believe in me?" he replies, "I believe in the Devil, but I also believe in the power of God for the same reason. And I also believe that the power of God is more powerful than that of the Devil." That is the moment he defeats and expels the devil. This is how a successful exorcism works.

Faith Protects Us from Evil

So, what was the key to the success of this exorcism? To expel the devil when it has possessed a person, it is important that the exorcist and the possessed person both have strong faith. If the possessed person has strong faith, the power of faith will work from within. Then, when combined with the external power of the exorcist's faith, the devil can be expelled. However, it is difficult to exorcise the devil if only one of them has faith. The key is for both to have strong faith.

I can expel the devil, or whichever demon it may be, as long as the person who is possessed has enough faith. However, if the possessed person believes more in the devil, or is on the devil's side and does not believe in El Cantare, even I cannot expel the demon unless it is an exceptional case. This is because the mind of the person is closer to the devil and the person becomes, in a way, a friend of it.

As you can see, if a person is on the devil's side, the devil will stay no matter how much help is offered from outside. When this happens, the person will experience a lot of misfortune, and we can do nothing except wait until the person becomes aware that his or her ideas and way of life need to be corrected.

People with faith do not become possessed by the devil

in the first place. In some cases, people of faith might have to face possession by a devil-class demon as a kind of trial of their faith. But if their faith is firm and unwavering, if they don't succumb to the temptations of worldly ideas such as "winning vs. losing," or "success vs. failure," the devil cannot continue to possess them for long.

For example, let us suppose that one of our believers runs in a national election. Even if he does not get elected because many people did not trust him, he must not feel discouraged or lose his faith just because a miracle didn't occur. If that happens, and the devil possesses him and makes him ill, it might be difficult to save him.

Even if you suffer defeat in an election, you should think of it in the following way: "This is a test of the strength of my soul. We are making sacrifices to 'make straight the way of the Lord.' We are walking through a thorny patch to open up the path to success. So my heart will not waver because of this. My task is to increase the number of our supporters, people who trust our party and who want to join the Happy Science movement. Even if progress is slow, I will move forward step by step. I will not let my personal interests stop me from carrying out my tasks."

As long as you have this feeling in your heart, the devil will never overtake you. Remember, our path in this world is full of stones that we can easily trip on. Keep your faith strong, and do not let go of it, no matter what you stumble over.

CHAPTER 3

A New Era of Spirituality

Restoring Spirituality in Today's World

Over the course of history, we've seen a shift from an era of spirituality to the modern era of knowledge, information, and technology. But now we are entering a time of restoring spirituality. Various religious movements have attempted to restore spirituality throughout the last hundred years. However, the flow of modern civilization seems to have suppressed these religious movements.

Today, a growing number of people believe that worldly technology, knowledge, and accomplishments are more reliable, accurate, and direct ways of getting things done than religion. Amidst all this, the issue of whether people believe or do not believe in religion has lost its relevance, and all things religious have regressed.

Alchemy, an early form of religious belief, has also been on the wane globally for more than a century. Modern journalism tends to portray elements and concepts related to alchemy as if they were the characteristics of a cult. The media are predisposed to cement the belief that nothing can defy the common rules of this world. But this is just a matter of differences in our perspectives.

Unknown things are always mysterious to people. For example, upon the invention of television, people couldn't believe that a machine in the shape of a box could display images, transmit sounds and relay information. When the telegraph was introduced in Japan, some people tied packages to the power lines, believing the telegraph could deliver them.

Some consider the mystical aspects of religion "old" and obsolete simply because they have existed since primitive times. These people seem to think that they can enter a new era if they do away with these "old" ideas.

For example, most modern medical practitioners believe that they can't save a sick person unless they replace the body part, that removing the affected part is the only way to cure the illness, and that the sick can only survive if they take medication for the remainder of their lives. This kind of materialistic thinking has become the norm in the field of medicine. Because they don't believe in the mystical power of faith, hospitals today treat the human body as if it were a machine that has broken down. This is especially true in the treatment of serious diseases.

About twenty years ago, Happy Science was not known as a religion that cured illnesses, nor was doing so part of my plans. I thought that going to a hospital to receive treatment or medication was a faster, more efficient way to cure a disease than going to a religion. At the time, I thought that it would be better for my organization to focus on its doctrines and stay away from curing illnesses. Perhaps my academic and professional background had something to do with this.

Back then, I had an interview with Mr. Shoichi Watanabe, an English scholar and cultural critic. I remember him saying that he didn't know of any religion that openly declared that it did not intend to cure illnesses. The modern, rational life I lived then may have had too great an influence on me.

Today, it is increasingly difficult for people who are involved in the most advanced fields of work and study to develop a pure and open heart. Their knowledge stands as an obstacle that blocks the pipeline of communication with Heaven. They have developed "horizontal connections" to communicate with others on Earth, but their "vertical connections" to communicate with Heaven are not functioning.

Through a number of spiritual messages and other spiritual phenomena, I have been proving the existence of the vertical connections between Heaven and Earth. When we connect with Heaven, we can receive spiritual light or messages from our guardian and guiding spirits. At first, I was the only one who could provide such proof of spiritual connection. But recently, my disciples have also begun to learn to do this.

In principle, creating a connection between Heaven and Earth is not difficult—you simply need to accept God's Truths. However, sometimes we cannot see these Truths clearly enough. When mist forms on a glass window, light cannot fully penetrate it. In the same way, dust and mist accumulate on the windows of our hearts while we live in this world. We must clear them away through self-reflection and increase the clarity of our hearts so that the light of Heaven illuminates us.

Successive Mystical Phenomena Are the Proof of Miracles

The reasoning of people who deny the occurrence of spiritual phenomena is not very consistent. It is actually quite weak. Often, these people can only say, "I've never seen nor heard them." Their reason for denying the existence of the spirit world is often that they have not witnessed the spiritual phenomena themselves.

Unlike mathematics, spiritual phenomena do not always yield the same results. It is not like a chemical experiment in which we ignite a mixture of hydrogen and oxygen to create water. Nor do we aim to obtain the same results every time. The modern world may regard the spirit world as a "lost world." But if we were to show even one, two, or three examples of real spiritual phenomena, all grounds for denying the existence of the spirit world would crumble.

Take, for instance, the dominant theory about the extinction of the dinosaurs. It states that 65 million years ago, a large meteorite fell on the Yucatan Peninsula and produced tons of dust that covered the Earth so densely and for such an extended period of time that solar rays could not penetrate the atmosphere. Plants no longer grew, and the dinosaurs starved to death. The only surviving animals were small rodent-like mammals, which, they believe, are linked to modern man through a long period of evolution.

We would not need to bring together every possible piece of evidence to disprove this theory. If we found just one dinosaur in Loch Ness, off the coast of New Zealand, or in the Sea of Japan, then, in a moment, all hypotheses affirming that dinosaurs only lived in prehistoric times and died off more than 65 million years ago would no longer be valid. Likewise, many people assert that extraterrestrials do not exist, but if we could capture one single UFO and prove that it was not fabricated by humans, that theory would be overturned.

In the same way, anyone can assert that religion cannot

cure illnesses. Not only doctors and scientists, but also the mass media and members of the general public can claim that it is a lie to say that faith heals diseases. However, if we can identify only one or two instances in which faith cured an illness that doctors claimed was incurable and that the patient would certainly die, the effect would be similar. The grounds for denial would break down, and the hypothesis that religion *can* cure diseases would be proven valid.

Many people may not believe or give credit to the spiritual laws of curing illnesses that I am preaching now. Under the laws of this material world on Earth, there are some instances in which faith cannot cure someone who is sick. But if we can show a series of instances of spiritual healings or mystical phenomena, that would be enough to prove wrong those who claim that faith cannot cure illnesses.

At Happy Science, we have long stated that many miracles shall occur when our faith becomes stronger. And just as we said, we have actually been seeing many miracles recently. For example, after my lecture at the celebration of my birthday in July 2011[1], the organizers showed a video of a Happy Science member who had fully recovered from terminal cancer through studying my teachings of God's Truths, reflecting on his thoughts and deeds, and praying at

---

1. This lecture has been compiled in Chapter 5 of this book.

the Happy Science temples.

Additionally, in recent reports, I have read testimonies about cancer, aortic aneurysms, pulmonary edemas and other serious diseases that faith has cured. Another report tells of a member whose finger healed after a dog almost tore it to pieces. Other accounts of spiritual healing also exist. Religion is certainly nothing to look down upon.

It is important that we keep providing proof as one after another example arises. Again, if someone claims he has seen a dinosaur and even has a photo to prove it, the skeptics will tell him, "I do not believe in something that I didn't see with my own eyes," or "The dinosaur in the photo is not real. It is just a model of a dinosaur." However, if we catch one dinosaur in Loch Ness, another in a lake in Japan, another in Lake Baikal, and one more in the Pacific Ocean, even these people would no longer be able to deny that dinosaurs exist.

The general public would probably find it hard to believe this, but in actual fact, when the great earthquake hit the eastern part of Japan, the tsunami avoided hitting houses and areas where Happy Science members lived. If a similar situation arises again, and if a tsunami avoids hitting the houses of our members again, then those who are skeptical now may start believing in miracles. I believe that a series of successive mystical phenomena will provide concrete proof of the power of faith.

Miracles Are God's Answers to the Faithful

In churches, temples, and other places on Earth, religious leaders teach what faith is. But even those who are praying in churches probably cannot be completely sure if the other world really exists, if God really exists, and if the divine beings and angels that assist God really exist.

The unexpected occurrences of unworldly miraculous phenomena are, in fact, the answers to those with faith. Just as you get a response when you knock on a door, you can receive an answer to your faith. Such miraculous phenomena are gradually increasing in number. The more people have faith, the more miracles will occur.

In this world, innumerable invisible electrical waves are transmitted everywhere. So too are the thoughts of hundreds of millions of people. When the majority of people share worldly views based on what modern science and conventional ideas tell them, their thoughts can prevent miracles from occurring. But when more people become aware of the miracles that occur at Happy Science and believe that miracles do happen, then their faith will create an energy field that will trigger miracles.

Even in this three-dimensional material world, we can create unworldly spaces, like portals to a different dimension, as spots for triggering miracles. These spaces could be, for example, local Happy Science temples or our main temples. Mystical phenomena occur at these trans-dimensional spots.

Various spiritual phenomena also occur when Happy Science members watch a video or listen to an audio recording of my lectures. The devoted members of Happy Science (who pledge their dedication to the Three Treasures) can obtain a CD that contains my recitation of our main sutra, "Buddha's Teaching: The Dharma of the Right Mind." I often teach the benefits of "The Dharma of the Right Mind." I myself have actually experienced the great power of this sutra and use it for various purposes.

Whenever I feel sad, heavy, or frustrated for no particular reason, I play the CD of "The Dharma of the Right Mind." When I turn up the volume on the CD, I can quickly sense what is disturbing me and identify what the problem is. For example, I might realize that one of the management staff is in trouble and wants help. This doesn't necessarily mean that people's souls have traveled to me; rather, it is their thoughts that come to me. Sometimes I pick up the thoughts of people I have met at places where I have preached or on the street or in various other places. In most cases, they come to me with a problem. They usually leave once I solve their problems, and they feel satisfied with my answers. This is an example of the spiritual phenomena I experience.

"The Dharma of the Right Mind" is particularly effective at exposing the evil spirits that cause illnesses by perpetually attaching themselves to a sick person. Evil spirits suffer when they hear "The Dharma of the Right Mind." So if you repeatedly play the CD, you will be able to make the evil spirits eventually leave the sick person.

This CD is so effective that sometimes, evil spirits become uncomfortable and leave as soon as I even think about playing the CD, before I take any action. But simply listening to "The Dharma of the Right Mind" is still a passive action. If you can make it a habit to earnestly study the teachings of the Truths and deepen your understanding of them, you can increase the effectiveness of this sutra.

The Spirit World Is Just as Real Now As It Was in Ancient Times

Buddhism teaches that everybody must strive to become a *buddha*. Of course, it would be difficult, if not impossible, to become the Great Buddha. But it is possible for everyone to be awakened, which is another meaning of becoming a buddha.

In a sense, you reach the first stage of enlightenment when you awaken to the spiritual Truths and realize that you are spiritual existence. You will realize that the vibrations of your mind attract evil spirits when they are in the wrong direction and attract angels when they are in the right direction. You will also understand that the other world and this world are not completely separate, but are, in fact, inextricably and closely linked, like two sides of the same coin, and that they interact with each other. You need to realize that this is not just an ancient philosophy. This is what it means to be awakened to spirituality.

Ancient people believed in spiritual resurrection, yet they also feared that the dead might come back as zombies. They were worried that the dead might emerge from their graves and chase them, much like Jiang Shis (reanimated corpses, in Chinese folklore) that are equivalent to demons in ancient civilizations. The ancients often folded the hands and broke the feet of the dead and placed heavy stones directly on top of their bellies so that the dead could never come out again.

In the old days, people commonly believed that the dead had three possible destinations: to return to Heaven and rest in peace, to fall to Hell, or to become stray spirits and remain in the earthly world. This may seem like an old belief, but even today, those who have died may not be able to rest in peace simply by having a funeral.

We are in an era of advanced technology, and television, the Internet, and cell phones have all spread throughout the world. But our technology does not negate this view of the afterworld. Instead, television, the Internet, cell phones, and the like are modern tools that actually help us prove the existence of the invisible world.

It is truly incredible that we can interact and exchange messages and pictures with people on the other side of the world. Similar interactions are actually possible in the spirit world. In fact, I perceive the thoughts of different people every day. I can hear their voices, and I can even see those who send intensive and concentrated thoughts to me. I also frequently talk with different spirits in Heaven, particularly in the early hours of the morning. Today, the scientific technology has brought the workings of this material world closer to how things work in the spirit world. I want everyone to recognize that advanced technology does not disprove the existence of the spirit world.

The proof that the era of spirituality is here can come in many forms. Some people might miraculously recover from chronic disease, while others might experience spiritual phenomena such as hearing the voices of spirits and experiencing the warm light that comes from Heaven. Some people might see gold dust falling from the sky.

In numerous cases, people have achieved extraordinary results that were above and beyond their capabilities. Some people have experienced non-coincidental encounters with others and have felt that some invisible power must be guiding them. These types of phenomena prove that various invisible forces are operating on Earth and that help comes from the spirit world.

The laws of the mind will always be at work, no matter how much our material civilization advances. No one can change the laws of the mind; nor can anyone change the spiritual rule that humans reincarnate between this world and the other world based on the laws of the mind. Please remember this.

Physical Readings and Space-People Readings

I use a range of spiritual powers, and I am likely one of the people in the world who possesses the highest level of spiritual power. I have spiritual powers equivalent to the Six Divine Powers in Buddhism, and I can conduct past-life readings and karma readings using my ability of clairvoyance.

For example, I can look into a person's past life, before he or she was born in this world, and establish the cause of difficult health problems that he or she suffers in the present life; for example, allergies. I can also see through people's bodies, as if I were a CT scan or a human X-ray, and tell them where they have problems.

Furthermore, I can talk with the consciousnesses of organs. Doctors would be astounded to hear this, but for me, it is like talking to a person. I can speak to the consciousness of the kidney, for example, and ask it why it got sick. I can hear its response and find the cause of illness. If doctors saw me having conversations with organs, they would probably be disturbed. Yet, reading the body, or the physical reading, is genuinely one of my spiritual abilities.

Another type of reading I frequently conduct at Happy Science is space-people readings. Many channelers (mediums) around the world claim to have received a message from space aliens or to be able to hear their words. I have read these kinds of books, but they completely lack any description of the extraterrestrial planets. This makes me question whether they really are hearing the words of space people. In most cases, these channelers are simply conveying the words of earth spirits that identify themselves as extraterrestrials.

On the other hand, the space-people readings we conduct at Happy Science are an extension of the past-life readings that I explained earlier. These readings search deep into the memories of people who are living on Earth now; we go back thousands, hundreds of thousands, even millions of years to explore the history of the soul before it arrived on Earth. This reading goes beyond time and space and recalls the memory of the soul from the time when it still resided in outer space. Like entering a wormhole, we slip into another time, recall the person's consciousness from another era, and have a conversation with it.

This type of reading is possible because I am able to trace the memory very far back, farther than what is usually achievable in past-life readings. You may ask how I can do this. It may sound a bit outdated, but it is similar to playing back the music of a gramophone record. If we can establish a connection with the old part of the soul, we can "play back" that memory. This is how I have been bringing back the ancient memories of various people who have lived in outer space, and allow their souls to come to life through their spiritual messages.

At the present moment, I have never heard of any other cases of space-people readings done in this way. Some people may claim that this is not possible, but we cannot change the fact that we actually can and have done it.

Using Spiritual Power
To Perform Exorcisms and Cure Illnesses

In addition to conducting space-people readings and conversing with spirits, I can also draw in the light of Heaven and emit it at will. If you can receive God's light or the light of Heaven at will, then you also should be able to emit that light at will. However, people tend to develop an inclination towards being either passive or active. Those who are dynamic and active often have difficulty taking a passive role. On the other hand, some people in our group who are capable of receiving spiritual messages find that their ability is often limited to hearing the voice of spirits, and they are not particularly good at taking the active role of emitting spiritual light.

In my case, I often use my hands to conduct spiritual readings and emit spiritual light. I also can perform exorcisms by drawing in spiritual power and emitting it from my hands. By casting a strong spiritual light, I can expel the evil spirit that possesses a person.

When you acquire the ability to do this, you will also be able to cure illnesses by expelling the evil spirits that are causing the illnesses. However, when the evil spirit has something to say, you need to listen to the reason why it connected with that person in the first place and then persuade it to leave. It is very difficult to expel evil spirits unless you can get them to agree to leave. In order to talk evil spirits into leaving, you must deepen your wisdom and acquire a certain level of understanding of the Truths.

Some evil spirits are extremely powerful and aggressively attack us. They are called devils. These beings wait for the slightest chance to attack religious organizations and spiritual leaders because they would lose their place in Hell if God's Truths were to spread in this world. In these cases, we may face extremely fierce battles.

Given the slightest chance, devils can attack even those of fine character who have a pure heart. An example of this is the old story of Jesus undergoing forty days of ascetic training in the wilderness. When Jesus was suffering from hunger, the devil Beelzebub appeared and tempted Jesus to transform the stone into bread to prove that he was the son of God. Beelzebub also tried to trick Jesus by telling him to jump off the top of the temple since an angel would come to save him, if, in fact, he was the son of God, as the Old Testament prophesized. These stories are contained in the New Testament (Matt. 4:1-11).

Shakyamuni Buddha also had a similar experience, according to the Buddhist scriptures. One day, he went out to ask for alms (food), but as it was a festival day, not many people were in the village, and he didn't receive anything.

He was returning home with an empty bowl when a devil came and tempted him to try one more house and told him that this time, Shakyamuni would receive something for sure. Of course, if you do not have anything to eat, you become hungry and can even become obsessive about food. The devil took advantage of such a situation to tempt Shakyamuni.

Devils are really spiteful. They use extremely mean and vicious tactics and attack our weaknesses. Devils wait for the small troubles that occur in our daily lives, and use them as opportunities to delude us into the wrong path. To fight off devils, we need a strong spiritual power to reject their temptations and dispel them.

After a few years of spiritual training within our group, you will gain the power to cure illnesses, perform exorcisms, and conduct spiritual readings. I believe that the number of people who acquire this power will gradually increase.

While Jesus was alive, he did almost all the work, and his disciples hardly exercised their spiritual powers. His disciples looked up to him, but they were unable to perform miracles themselves. After Jesus's death and resurrection, however, they acquired the spiritual power to do what Jesus did while he was alive. The disciples became able to cure illnesses, speak in foreign tongues, and experience many other spiritual phenomena.

Of course, the forces from the spirit world were at work

to some extent, but the disciples' faith was the main and essential force that worked the miracles. Seeing the Resurrection of Jesus, the disciples gained strong faith in Jesus, and their faith gave them the power to perform miracles themselves. These miracles led them to start missionary work on a large scale and eventually created impassioned missionaries that spread Christianity worldwide.

Strong Faith Overturns Disbelief

Spirituality is not an outdated theme. Rather, it is the most important concept for people living today. The original mission of philosophy was to seek answers to the fundamental questions: "What are humans?" and "What is the essential nature of human beings?" However, modern philosophy has not fulfilled this mission. Neither does modern science, which is still bogged down in the theory that human beings are like machines. But now, Happy Science is providing clear answers to these questions.

Those of us who believe in the power of faith should never feel discouraged. We need to continue steadily advancing forward. You shouldn't hesitate from your mission even if someone claims that there is no concrete proof that religion can cure illnesses. Remember the example of the dinosaurs. If only one Lock Ness monster is found alive, the grounds for denial of their existence would automatically crumble. Likewise, even one instance of religion curing a disease that doctors deemed incurable will negate their theory that religion cannot cure illnesses. I believe it is important that we build up evidence of these cases.

The power of disbelief is still too strong, which is why our missionary work in Japan is not progressing as much as we hoped it would. Considering the amount of effort and activity we have put into Japan, we haven't seen enough increase in those who have faith. This is probably because society is currently dominated by ideas that deny the possibility of miracles of faith.

The conventional ideas taught by mass education are deeply rooted in people's minds. People have been deluded into thinking that those who believe in such miracles are unsophisticated and unintelligent. We must prove that this is not the case, and become the powerful force that will foster miracles.

The accepted disbelief in religion has escalated into a powerful force that prevents miracles of faith from happening. We must overturn this accepted disbelief. Being the minority, we need to have unwavering faith to push forward our belief. Bearing this firmly in mind, it is my hope that we keep striving forward to open a new era of spirituality.

CHAPTER 4

The Arrival
Of the New Space Age

Learning about Space People

In the process of conducting many space-people readings and publishing them, I have gathered abundant evidence of the existence of space people as well as detailed information about them.

My experience with space people reminds me of the earlier experiences I had. Between 1981 and 1986, before I founded Happy Science, I recorded and transcribed spiritual messages from Divine Spirits in Heaven. I would read the transcripts, analyze every detail, and wonder to myself, "Could this really be Nichiren?" "Could this really be Kūkai[1]?" "Could this really be Jesus?" Now, twenty-five years later, my research has taken me into the cosmic universe.

---

1. Kūkai was a Japanese monk who founded the Shingon or "True Word" school of Buddhism (774–835). Kūkai is famous as a calligrapher and engineer and was also a civil servant, scholar, poet, and artist.

Back in the 1980s, when I was recording the spiritual messages, I remember feeling amazed that I could talk with the Divine Spirits of prominent historical figures. Now, I find it equally astonishing that I can summon the past lives of souls before they became earth people—when they lived in outer space—and engage them in an ongoing dialogue in real time.

A lot of you have probably imagined that extraterrestrial life exists somewhere in the universe. Now I am beginning to reveal to you, little by little, detailed information about who they are, what they look like, and how they think.

This investigation into space people began with random fragments of information. But gradually, these pieces of information have begun to reveal the connections between different types of space people. Some pieces are still missing, but we are beginning to see the whole picture.

This process is similar to completing a jigsaw puzzle. Imagine that you are putting together a jigsaw puzzle of Earth. As you work on it, a partial picture begins to appear, and you might wonder, "Is this Africa?" "Could this be Australia?" "This looks like the United States." This is the stage my research is at right now. The puzzle is not complete yet, but I am on the brink of connecting different pieces of information together.

The Mechanisms of Space-People Readings

To gather information about beings from outer space, I use a method called space-people readings, which I only discovered recently. I do not fully understand the mechanisms of these readings yet myself, so I cannot describe exactly how this method works and why it is possible.

As I often mention, after people die and return to the other world, they are shown a one- or two-hour film about their lives. It is like a biographical movie, or a roundup of the most memorable scenes of a person's life, and it reveals what kind of life the person lived on Earth. If you gather just its most significant incidents, a life of eighty years or more can be summarized into a film about one or two hours long. A group of people watch the film and give their overall impression of the person's time on Earth, which determines the person's destination in the afterlife.

In the case of space-people readings, the scope extends beyond a single human life. The reading condenses the soul's history from the very beginning, from its creation in outer space through its current earthly life. From that span, I focus only on the part of the soul that lived in outer space, and play back those memories like a film. As a result, the soul's space-being consciousness comes alive, enabling it to share its thoughts.

In the present day, you cannot change the story or the contents of a movie while you are watching it. But in the future, I think that we will have interactive movies that will allow the audience to engage in live conversations with the characters they are watching.

For instance, during a battle scene between a cowboy and aliens, an audience member will be able to raise his or her hand and shout, "Hey, let me ask you something!" and the cowboy would turn around and reply, "Howdy, stranger, what is it?" The person in the audience would ask, "You're just a cowboy. How come you can fight aliens?" And the cowboy would answer, "Because my weapon has a special gadget that can shoot down that UFO when I aim at a certain part of it."

We are presently witnessing a shift from 2D to 3D movies. Further technological advancement should soon make it possible to reenact history and historical events, so that we can experience them as if they were happening in the present. With current technological developments already headed in this direction, the age of interactive movies should arrive within a few decades.

My space-people readings work in a similar fashion as interactive movies might work. Although we are watching images from the past, we can converse with the space-people characters within them because their souls are still alive. When I do space-people readings, the consciousness of the living person I am conducting the reading on will reach back into his or her memory of life in outer space and describe bygone events. This is how we can trace back and reproduce the memories of souls as far back as thousands, hundreds of thousands, and even millions of years ago.

Another way of explaining my space-people readings is by comparing them to time travel, a phenomenon that souls from outer space have described quite frequently. Even the closest star to Earth is at least four light-years away, which means that traveling to Earth would take a minimum of four years at the speed of light. More distant stars are millions or hundreds of millions of light years away from our planet. So even at the speed of light, it would take forever to travel such distances.

It is hard to imagine that the inhabitants of a star one hundred million light years away would travel one hundred million years to come to Earth. A more likely explanation for time travel is the use of cosmic wormholes, which are special tunnels in the universe that can compress space and time. When space people from far-off planets travel through wormholes, they cover not only great distances but also millions of years of time as well.

In our dialogues with space people, they often have difficulty identifying the exact dates when certain events took place. I believe this has something to do with their travels through wormholes.

In one of the ancient Japanese myths, a few days in the palace of the sea gods were equivalent to several centuries on Earth. But if extraterrestrial beings had to travel across time and space in a spaceship, it would be possible that one hundred million, five hundred million, or even a billion years on Earth would have passed by the time they arrived on our planet. In this sense, space people are not only travelers from the ancient past, but also denizens of the present. In the cosmic universe, such seeming contradictions do exist.

Some of you may remember the story of the first film in the *Planet of the Apes* series, where astronauts exploring outer space stumble upon an unknown planet. There, they find, half buried in the sand, the Statue of Liberty, and discover that the desolate location was formerly New York City. They realize that the planet they had come upon was, in fact, planet Earth—but in the future, and that a very long time had passed while they were traveling in outer space. So much time, in fact, that the human race was almost extinct, and apes had evolved into the dominant species. This is actually very possible. By the same token, people could travel in a time machine to the distant future, but the distant future they reach could be exactly the same point in time where they started.

The underlying principles of time travel and space navigation are probably closely related. Once we solve the mystery of time and space, we will be able to explain the mechanisms of traveling across time and space.

It is theoretically possible to travel physical distances instantly and to travel to different points in time. Time is often described as a circular or a spiral movement. It doesn't necessarily advance in a straight, linear fashion. It goes back and forth and round and round in circles much like the lines in a snail's shell. Therefore, if you can locate the coordinates of the day or the era to which you would like to travel, it should be possible to travel across time. Space scientists and astrophysicists need to explore this further. I believe that, in the future, the principles of astrophysics and the teachings of new religion will integrate.

The Power of Clairvoyance

Although I cannot provide a thorough explanation of how it works, I know that it is possible to access the past, present, and future in an instant. This might not be possible for everyone, but I can see the past, present, and future as a single point so small that it could fit in the palm of my hand. I also can see a single point in time as infinite.

Even a very long period of time, such as hundreds of millions of years, billions of years, or even tens of billions of years, can condense into a single point. This could enable us to travel to any point in time we choose. In a sense, the future is already happening now. Similarly, the boundless universe can condense into a tiny point, or expand infinitely.

I have conducted a remote-viewing investigation of Area 51[2] in the Nevada desert, where the U.S. government presumably hides UFOs and extraterrestrials. So it stands to reason that I may be able to conduct remote viewing of the future as well.

If I focus my attention on a specific location, time, and topic in the future, I can probably see events in the future. For example, if someone asks me, "What is going to happen in the year 3100 in this particular location, concerning this particular issue?" I could focus my attention and visually see what is happening at that location, about that issue, 1,088 years from now. I also can probably remotely view what kind of civilization is going to exist on a specific star a thousand years from now. I haven't engaged in this activity yet, but I believe I am blessed with this skill.

This is actually the power of enlightenment. Now, I

---

2. Master Okawa conducted and recorded a remote viewing investigation of Area 51 on August 4, 2011.

am about to enter a world of enlightenment beyond time and space. This is one of the characteristics of El Cantare's enlightenment, which indeed surpasses both Shakyamuni Buddha's enlightenment and Jesus Christ's enlightenment.

Space People Reveal Secrets behind
The Genesis Story

Many channelers today—not only in Japan but also in other countries such as Britain and the United States—claim that they can hear the voices of entities who identify them-selves as extraterrestrials. The question about these voices is whether they are really coming from space people or from somewhere in the spirit world.

To the best of my knowledge, none of the books featur-ing messages from space aliens offer anything beyond the spiritual messages I have recorded so far. Many of these writings also resemble the internationally published spiritual messages from Silver Birch and White Eagle, entities from the spirit world who use ancient Native American names to communicate with people on Earth. Little difference exists between Silver Birch's and White Eagle's messages and the communications that reportedly emanate from space beings.

Although many people claim to hear the voices of space

aliens, their descriptions of the aliens' home stars are much too simple. They are unable to offer any details, and their descriptions sound like made-up stories invented on the spot. Information at this level could easily stem from Earth's spirit group. I do not believe that these writings provide sufficient evidence that they came from space people.

On the other hand, each of the space-people readings that I have conducted has supplied interrelated information. Now that we have completed many of them, we will need to prove their authenticity. As I conduct more readings, the large quantity of information on the subject will transform into a high quality of information. It is not usually possible for a single person to fabricate a large number of fake testimonials, one after another. As long as we keep providing authentic readings, sooner or later we will be able to see the whole picture clearly.

In recent years, I have discovered that we have particularly strong connections with the stars Pleiades and Vega. I am not sure whether these stars are connected with the planet Earth in general or with Happy Science in particular, but they have been exerting a strong influence on us. We also have learned that their roots are closely connected with the civilization that once flourished on Venus.

In my book *The Laws of the Sun*, I wrote that the roots of humankind on Earth trace back to a civilization on

Venus, and that the entity now known to us as El Cantare was known on Venus as El Miore. Through space-people readings, we are now discovering many things that *The Laws of the Sun* did not explain, including the fact that El Cantare, or El Miore, has sent down portions of his soul to guide life on various stars.

It seems that portions of the El Cantare spirit or his brother souls have taken physical form on the stars that have strong bonds with Happy Science, such as Pleiades and Vega. It is even possible that the core consciousness of El Cantare actually descended onto these stars. We probably will learn the truths of this history as my future teachings gradually reveal more about the laws of the universe. For example, we might hear stories about El Cantare when he lived on Pleiades and Vega.

Before we move on to that stage, however, more people need to understand that the universe is full of space people —space brothers and sisters and star people—who have established their own civilizations on their own stars and planets. Once people accept this fact, it will serve as the foundation for the new knowledge I will provide, and I will then be able to tell the story of El Cantare's incarnations on other stars.

In a sense, these stories compare to the mythical elements that characterize most religions. All religions have creation myths, which, from a modern interpretation, are shrouded in mystery. Still, some of the very mythical aspects of traditional creation stories might actually contain truth, rendering them still very relevant today.

I am now starting to teach a new genesis on a cosmic scale. This will become valuable knowledge for us as we try to see the future of humanity. Knowing that a plethora of civilizations exist on other planets throughout the cosmic universe will show us that our future holds limitless potential for progress.

The Origins of Human and Animal Life

A considerable number of human beings on Earth originated from outer space. Some immigrated to Earth as space people and gradually assimilated to human life. Others came to Earth as souls and dwelled in human bodies. Space people have found many ways to become earth people.

We also have gathered evidence that the ancestors of some animals came to Earth from outer space in physical form. Through my readings, I have found many creatures in outer space that are similar to Earth's pets and farm animals. At this stage, however, I cannot be certain that every type of life form found on Earth exists in other habitats in outer space; there are some animals that I have not yet found in outer space. So it is difficult to theorize that all animals on our planet came from outer space on a spaceship like Noah's Ark. I suppose that some animals originated on Earth and others evolved on Earth into different forms. Consequently, I have to say that Darwin's generally accepted theory of evolution is half correct and half mistaken.

According to Darwin's theory of evolution, the first life was born when an accumulation of proteins gained motion. Then, microorganisms appeared and gradually evolved into the amphibians, reptilians, birds, and mammals that we know today. However, if you study my space-people readings, you will see that this theory is incorrect. Reptiles, birds, and mammals did not separate from the evolutionary tree. Actually, they came to Earth from outer space at some point in our planet's history.

Our space-people readings found beings that look like deer, rabbits, squirrels, pigs, and capybaras[3] on different stars. We also have accumulated a lot of evidence that many reptile-like animals have come to Earth. Once here, some of them kept their original form, while others became larger or smaller, or acquired new features.

---

3. The capybara is the largest living rodent in the world. Capybaras are native to South America and live on the banks of rivers and lakes.

The dinosaurs, for example, now considered extinct, found such ample supplies of food within Earth's warm climate that they increased greatly in size. Fossils prove that dinosaurs were several dozen meters tall at the prime of their existence. But according to space-people readings, they were much smaller when they first arrived on our planet. They were once only a few meters tall, but their bodies gradually evolved into the giant creatures we know. I also believe that some dinosaur species, which originally arrived as reptile-like animals, eventually evolved into humans.

I would like to dedicate more research to this subject in the future. What I know for certain at this stage is that modern scientists are wrong in claiming that life first sprang from an accumulation of proteins, developed into mouse-like creatures, and eventually evolved into human beings. In this sense, Darwin's theory of evolution is incorrect. However, it is probably true that beings from outer space went through a form of evolution in the process of adapting to the new environment on Earth.

Speaking of dinosaurs, no conclusive evidence exists that they have become extinct. Since the oceans are vast, the chances for ships to stumble across one of these creatures are very low. Yet, there have been occasional sightings of giant sea creatures, and unidentifiable animal corpses have been found out at sea. So it is quite possible that giant sea creatures could still exist today. It might be interesting for me to examine Loch Ness through spiritual remote viewing. But as Loch Ness covers a huge area and is extremely deep, it would be a very time-consuming endeavor to search the whole lake for the existence of a large water creature.

In any case, space-people readings have revealed the secrets of the theory of evolution, identifying which parts are true, and which parts are false. Furthermore, they have showed that the creation myth of the human race as told in the Biblical Genesis story is partially true: human beings were created on Earth. But at the same time, space-people readings show that a portion of the human race also originated from outer space.

A Folktale of an Encounter with Space People

Ancient Japanese myths describe how gods built Japan from a stair-like bridge called Ama-no-uki-hashi, which connects the world of the gods, Takama-ga-hara, with this world. In these myths, there is no clear distinction between Takama-ga-hara and this world, and the gods cross the bridge, back and forth. They also depict gods flying in spaceship-like aircrafts called Ama-no-torifune.

Certain ancient Japanese folktales make us suspect that

they could be describing interactions with beings from outer space. For example, the classic Japanese story of Princess Kaguya, or *The Tale of the Bamboo Cutter*, seems to be a legend of an encounter with a being from outer space.

The Tale of the Bamboo Cutter goes as follows:

One day, an elderly man was cutting bamboo in a bamboo grove when he noticed a shining light inside one of the stalks. When he came closer, he discovered a beautiful little girl, only about ten centimeters tall, sitting inside it. He took her home and took care of her. In just three months, the girl grew quickly into a beautiful young lady of ordinary size. She was beautiful like a princess, so they named her "Princess Kaguya." One day, Princess Kaguya suddenly said, "When the next full moon comes, I must return to the moon. People from the moon will come to take me back." As she predicted, the moon people came and took her away in a carriage on top of a shining cloud, as depicted in picture scrolls of *The Tale of the Bamboo Cutter*. The guards were sent to protect Princess Kaguya, but when they tried to fire arrows from the roof, they found themselves paralyzed and could not move.

This story closely resembles the many recent reports of abductions by space aliens. In these reports, victims have said that their bodies became completely immobilized and they found themselves at the mercy of their abductors. This suggests that *The Tale of the Bamboo Cutter* is based on actual events.

Another thing that suggests that Princess Kaguya might have been a being from outer space is that she was extremely small when the old man found her, but then grew to the size of a human adult within a very short space of time.

Beings from Vega have told us in space-people readings that they are capable of changing into any form they want. It is also possible that very small elf-like space people exist. When I was a child, numerous small UFOs about thirty centimeters in diameter were sighted in Kōchi Prefecture, a neighboring prefecture of my birthplace, Tokushima. Many photographs documented them. If space people resided inside those tiny UFOs, they would have to be very small, like Princess Kaguya when she was inside the stalk of the bamboo shoot. So it is very likely that this type of space being exists.

Happy Science and the Secrets of the Universe

Ever since I started teaching the laws of the universe two years ago, at the beginning of 2010, I have revealed them at a good pace. If I keep up the pace for another three years, I will probably be able to uncover even deeper mysteries of the universe.

Many people are still skeptical of the Truths I teach about the spirit world, yet now I am starting to unravel the mysteries of outer space. Even though many people are unconvinced that the spirit world exists, I am trying to guide them through the world of outer space. This would not be possible without the public trust in and support for Happy Science.

As with any religion, the mystical aspects of my teachings have drawn criticism, but this is simply a matter of faith. You can choose either to believe or not to believe. I would like to avoid the risks of these criticisms, which, in extreme cases, could lead to persecution of the organization. Still, I intend to continue my research to the greatest extent possible without jeopardizing Happy Science.

At the same time, I believe it is our duty, as a religion, to offer teachings that contain goodness. I want to help people live proper, healthy, and meaningful lives so that they do not suffer from any behavioral problems or psychological harm. I also hope that my teachings will help them develop higher levels of spiritual awareness, grow into persons of noble character, and become leaders.

Happy Science needs to keep offering the universal Truths that are common to other religions. These teachings have built a foundation of public trust upon which I have been able to reveal the Truths about the multidimensional structure of the spirit world. Now, I am about to unveil the secrets of the universe—its structure and the principles that govern it. People are starting to recognize that what they dismissed as mere slogans are real facts.

Ever since I began expounding on the laws of the universe in recent years, some people may have felt that I have suddenly started to speak of absurd things. But these teachings have actually been part of Happy Science from the beginning.

I wrote the first edition of *The Laws of the Sun* twenty-five years ago, in 1986. The first chapter of the book is equivalent to the Genesis. It describes how space people came to Earth from outer space and how life was created on Earth, which at that time might have sounded absurd to many people.

I also have been revealing sacred mysteries about El Cantare since the beginning. I had already introduced the name El Cantare in the first edition of *The Laws of the Sun*. In the 1994 Japanese edition, I added the subtitle, "The Path to El

Cantare." I had also proclaimed the descent of El Cantare at Tokyo Dome in 1991.

While Happy Science teaches useful knowledge about faith and religion, morality, philosophy, and ethics, we have always had an esoteric and mystical side, too. We have gradually disclosed more mystic teachings as our group has grown and become better established.

When we build more confidence as a religious organization, we will be able to make remarks on any issue, including ones we have not yet touched upon. It is also very likely that the esoteric teachings of Happy Science will provide clues to future science.

Anyone would be able to become a millionaire if they could see the future of society. If you knew, for example, that a railroad was to be built along a certain route, you could buy the mountains designated for its construction and cash in on the money for this land. In the same way, knowing what industries will develop in the future could help you plan ahead and achieve outstanding accomplishments. I am now engaging in the important task of revealing mystical Truths so as to provide as many clues as I can about future society.

As I mentioned earlier, the two stars that are exerting the strongest influence on Happy Science today are Pleiades and Vega. The teachings of Pleiades focus on beauty, love, harmony, and to some degree, progress. These concepts are similar to the teachings that I emphasize at Happy Science.

Vega, on the other hand, seems to have a strong relationship to my esoteric teachings on the mystical power of the mind. Happy Science teaches a concept similar to the teaching that one thought leads to three thousand worlds;[4] that is, that your destiny and surroundings can change based on your state of mind. These profound Buddhist concepts seem to have roots in the teachings of Vega.

Vegans are also known for their ability to reflect people's appearances like mirrors. They show people what they want to see, and they project whatever form their observer takes. This is a trait that I, myself, possess. I've always felt that I have a tendency to show people what they desire to see. There is probably a part of me that has a Vegan aspect.

One of my teachings states that as the world inside your mind changes, the outside world will change, too. Depending on the state of your mind, the world around you changes, your destiny changes, and even your appearance changes. This could be a universal Truth that serves as a basis for life on Vega.

---

4. "One thought leads to three thousand worlds" is a principle taught by the Chinese Buddhist monk T'ien-t'ai Chih-i (538–597 CE). It states that your state of mind in this world will determine your destination in the next. It is also known as "Three thousand realms in a single thought moment."

I have been adapting the Truths taught in other parts of the cosmos to our planet and teaching them on Earth as God's Truths. My mission is to integrate the Truths taught in many parts of the universe, as well as the teachings from well-run civilizations in other parts of the cosmos. It is also my mission to teach cosmic justice and to preach about the nature of good and evil from the perspective of the entire universe.

I believe that, among the laws I teach during my life on Earth, the ones that no one else could ever discover will last for two thousand or even three thousand years. The everlasting Truths that I am now teaching probably make up a part of the laws of the universe.

My study of the laws of the universe has only just begun, and I intend to dedicate my life to exploring this subject as far as possible. This is of special importance since I believe that not many others will be capable of continuing my work after I pass away. Therefore, I will devote myself to this feat as much as I can.

In this chapter, I have shared what I have discovered thus far about the secrets of the universe. It is my earnest hope that Happy Science will achieve more growth and become well established, so that I will be able to provide more of these mystical teachings.

CHAPTER 5

The Time for Salvation Is Here

The Challenge of Guiding People All Over the World

The year 2011 marked several milestones for me. It was the fifty-fifth anniversary of my birth on Earth, the thirtieth anniversary of my Great Enlightenment, and the twenty-fifth anniversary of the establishment of Happy Science. As I reached these important turning points, I realized that I had only achieved about 30 percent of my mission on Earth. Although the realization of my final goal still lies in the future, I feel very grateful that I have achieved at least part of my life's mission so far.

Ever since I was born, I have worked towards fulfilling my mission in this world. Yet, I am fully aware that without the help of many, I could not have come this far, nor could I continue my work. I am deeply thankful to everyone who has contributed to making this possible.

I always tell myself that we cannot assume the role of guiding others just because we wish to. I truly believe that one cannot attain a position of leadership and accomplish great tasks without the support, trust, and approval of many people.

I continually voice my suggestions and opinions to the leaders of Japan and to the world. I am firm in my viewpoints, and sometimes I may sound harsh. However, I understand their difficult positions, and I deeply respect these leaders' daily efforts.

Responsibility for a country is an extraordinarily demanding task for anyone. Regardless of how distinguished a person may be, he or she sometimes may seem to fall short of expectations. But this is most often because of the enormity of their undertaking. For example, the president of the United States of America, no matter how talented and extraordinary he or she may be, may still appear inadequate at times and receive frequent criticism.

As a global spiritual leader, I always find it challenging to give clear guidelines for the entire world, to teach about its ideal state, and to point everyone in the right direction. Each nation has its own objectives. The happiness and fulfillment of one country may in turn cause unhappiness to people who live in other countries. It is indeed extremely challenging to show people of different countries the ideal path, to bring the greatest happiness to the most people, and at the same time, to help those who too often get left out of sharing in that happiness.

I have watched over the long history of humankind from Heaven, a world beyond Earth, and guided the creation of human history. I now have come down to Earth to teach people all over the world the ideal state to which they should aspire. This is indeed an extremely hard task to accomplish, and I personally feel the weight of this challenging mission.

Considering that the world population has reached seven billion, the influence of Happy Science is still very limited. Still, my teachings have circulated to more than ninety countries[1], and in each country, our members are very actively studying, practicing, and spreading my teachings in order to contribute to the creation of an ideal world in the future.

The Truths I teach are the power, sent from Heaven, to bring happiness to all life in this world. These Truths serve as the light that illuminates the path towards greater happiness on Earth. I am the one that will expel darkness from this world.

Everyone pursues happiness in their own ways, but at the same time, everyone also suffers pain and sorrow. Often, relationship problems cast shadows on people's minds and hearts and cause sadness or anger. This pertains not only to individuals but also to groups of people. Companies and

---

1. As of December 2011

countries around the world continuously pursue happiness. But in doing so, their efforts can sometimes cause unhappiness to other people or other countries.

Disharmony occurs when people care only about their own happiness and forget about others. Conflicts occur when people fail to consider how they can harmonize with others as they seek happiness for themselves.

I pray that all of you will develop your own unique character, enjoy a sense of achievement, and attain the state of true happiness. I know, however, that in that process, you will probably worry and suffer, and create friction in your relationships with others.

It is good that so many different types of people, opinions, and ideologies populate this planet. But these differences can escalate and cause confusion and disorder. Nevertheless, forcing one idea on everyone and thereby ignoring or suppressing all other conflicting opinions, ideologies, and beliefs creates even greater suffering and unhappiness.

That's why I'm telling you to always remember the existence of the supreme being in the world beyond this material world. We will be able to end conflicts on Earth when we realize that all people, societies, and nations are walking on the same path towards this supreme being. When you become aware of this Truth, you will be able to acknowledge others' efforts, work together, and learn from one another. You will also be able to experience the happiness of knowing that you are all companions on the path towards the supreme being.

We must also remain humble. In the last hundred years or so, science and technology have progressed significantly. Compared to people who lived one or two hundred years ago, we certainly have much more knowledge and information. If you traveled in a time machine to one hundred years in the past, people might worship you as a god. That is how advanced we are in terms of our amount of knowledge and the level of technology compared to a century ago. This is the fruit of our civilization's academic progress and technological advancement. I wonder, however, whether the seven billion people living today have better states of mind than those who lived a hundred or two hundred years ago.

We must not forget that human beings are essentially sacred souls that dwell in physical bodies. No matter how much knowledge, technology, or monetary income we gain, we cannot lose track of the progress of our inner being. If the way we live costs us the radiance of our souls, then humanity will have advanced in technology, but regressed on the evolutionary path of the soul.

Resolving Religious Conflicts

The world population has grown significantly in recent years, and I feel that Earth is now entering a period of great transformation. At this time of imminent change, it appears that the world religions founded 2000 or 2500 years ago have concluded their mission. They struggle because in modern society, they are no longer capable of saving people's souls.

Even Christianity, considered one of the most advanced religions today, follows the doctrines that Jesus taught more than two thousand years ago. It seems to be in trouble because it cannot provide answers for the issues people face today. Similarly, the teachings that Shakyamuni Buddha preached 2500 years ago don't necessarily solve the problems of modern society.

In the same way, the sayings of Muhammad, recorded in the Koran and Hadith about 1400 years ago, have caused a lot of contradictions and confusion in modern Muslim society. The teachings are too old to provide the proper perspective for living in today's world.

Now in this twenty-first century, many disagreements arise between people who believe in the 1400-year-old Muslim teachings and people who believe in the 2000-year-old Christian teachings. These disagreements have triggered confrontations and conflicts in different parts of the world.

If the founders of these religions were alive today, they would probably be able to adapt their teachings to today's society. They could forge new interpretations or suggest compromises on different points, thereby enabling people to live in harmony with each other. Religions that originated a long time ago, however, haven't been able to modify the words of their founders to meet the needs of people living today.

That is why I am here now to present new perspectives about humanity, society, nations, and the world. I am trying to integrate various religions, philosophies, ideologies, and perspectives, and reconcile their conflicting views. I continue to give lectures on a variety of topics so that people can learn different perspectives on the issues of the world.

I preach not only for those who live today, but also for future generations. All answers can be found within my words. The seeds for the future are already contained in my many books. People of the future—those who will be born five hundred, a thousand, or two thousand years from now—shall find answers to their questions within my words.

Faith in the Universal Truths
Will Unify the World

The world population keeps growing towards ten billion, which means that the variety of ideas and perspectives among people will only increase. With so many people freely offering their opinions, it can be increasingly hard for them to reach a consensus.

One of the most distinctive characteristics of democracy is the idea that society can prosper by adopting the opinions of the majority. However, this same system may create confusion and disorder when the population becomes too large. If we do not do something about the ever-increasing conflicts of opinion, I'm afraid that the democratic system will come to an end soon. In saying this, however, I absolutely do not mean that the seven billion people would be happier if a militaristic dictatorship or single-party tyranny were to control them.

As we protect fundamental human rights, we must realize that humans are sacred beings not because the laws that they created say so, nor because they were accidentally born on Earth, nor because they can create and use tools, unlike other animals. Human beings are sacred because they are children of God. Human beings must be guaranteed freedom and dignity because they are children of God. This is the basis of human rights.

With the power of our will, we can produce new inventions and change the world for the better. With the power of our will, we can write the future. This is the proof that human beings are children of God.

So, my message to all of you is as follows: we must overcome differences and find unity among different ideas. But this can never be done by tyrannical, autocratic, or oppressive force.

In the world beyond this world, the light of the universal Truths is always shining like the North Star. Although this light is beyond the reach of humans, we must keep on pointing true north, to the direction of the universal Truths. By believing in the sacred values of the unknown world—the world that transcends this one—we will be able to overcome differences in opinion, ideology, belief, race, skin color, and language, and unite as one.

Charting a Path for Humanity in the Future

I have been making efforts on my end to prevent wars in the current era. My thoughts, however, transcend far beyond present affairs. I am concerned with how I can guide as many people as possible in the right direction towards true happiness, now and into the future. My purpose is to leave teachings that will serve as guidelines for the people who will be born five hundred, a thousand, two thousand, or three thousand years from now. I need to continue providing the teachings of the Truths for the future of humankind, regardless of whether or not people today understand 100 percent of what I teach.

True wisdom is what humanity needs.
You must seek the Truths.
You must strive to spread the Truths.
You must have courage to shed light
On the darkness that tries to conceal the Truths.

You must take vigorous actions
To create a bright future.
You must not get trapped
In the failures or small successes of this world.

Regardless of your nationality,
It is the mission of those who spread my teachings
To continuously show the right direction
To future generations.

You may face political disputes

Or diplomatic imbroglio among yourselves.
You may face conflicting economic interests.
We cannot avoid these issues,
As long as we live in this world.
But we must make efforts to solve them.
We must use our wisdom to overcome them.

We must never forget that
Beyond the issues of this material world,
We are all one as children of God.

In the light of this fact,
I boldly state that
We must break free from today's conventional beliefs,
And take courage to live in the Truth.

I ask you to be strong,
To seek the Truths,
And to have courage to pursue,
Explore, and practice them.
Do not give in
To the darkness that tries to conceal the Truths.

Know that courage is part of virtue.
Gain wisdom and courage

And take action.

Know that your mission is to pave the way,
Not only for your own life,
But also for others.
Make it your mission
To light the way for future generations.

No matter which country you are in,
It is the mission
Of the chosen ones, who join
The spiritual movement of Happy Science,
To continue laying the foundation,
Day after day,
For those who have yet to be born on Earth,
For future generations,
And for the future survival and prosperity
Of humanity.

Together, we can fulfill this noble mission
For the future of humankind.

Afterword

A new era is approaching.
We, humankind, need to discard long-held values,
And face new realities.

We must develop an understanding
Of the spirit world,
Of miracles,
Of space people.

By believing in them,
We will experience a paradigm shift,
A new awakening to our identity as *earth people*.
You are about to walk through the door
To a new era

That will last thousands of years.
As the new era unfolds,
You will realize that my teachings,
The laws within this book,
Are the guiding light,
The North Star,
For future humankind.

Ryuho Okawa
Founder and CEO
Happy Science Group
December 2011

About the Author

MASTER RYUHO OKAWA started receiving spiritual messages from Heaven in 1981. Holy beings appeared before him with impassioned messages of urgency, entreating him to deliver God's words to Earth. Within the same year, Master Okawa's deepest subconscious awakened and revealed his calling to become a spiritual leader who is inspiring the world with the power of God's Truths. Through these conversations with divine beings and through profound spiritual contemplation, Master Okawa developed the philosophy that would become the core of his teachings. His communications with Heaven deepened his understanding of God's designs and intentions—how He created our souls, this world, the other world, and the Laws that are the very fabric of the universe. In 1986, Master Okawa founded Happy Science to share God's Truths and to help humankind overcome religious and cultural conflicts and usher in an era of peace on Earth. The universality and integrity of his spiritual teachings, delivered in his uniquely simple and pragmatic way, have attracted millions of readers and followers in over ninety countries. In addition to publishing over eight hundred books, Master Okawa has delivered nearly 1,700 talks and lectures, and continues to share God's Truths throughout the world.

About Happy Science

In 1986, Master Ryuho Okawa founded Happy Science, a spiritual movement dedicated to bringing greater happiness to humankind by overcoming barriers of race, religion, and culture and by working toward the ideal of a world united in peace and harmony. Supported by followers who live in accordance with Master Okawa's words of enlightened wisdom, Happy Science has grown rapidly since its beginnings in Japan and now extends throughout the world. Today, it has twelve million members around the globe, with faith centers in New York, Los Angeles, San Francisco, Tokyo, London, Sydney, Sao Paulo, and Seoul, among many other major cities. Master Okawa speaks weekly at Happy Science centers and travels around the world giving public lectures. Happy Science provides a variety of programs and services to support local communities and people in need. These programs include preschools, after-school educational programs for youths, and services for senior citizens and the disabled. Members also participate in social and charitable activities, which in the past have included providing relief aid to earthquake victims in Chile, China, and Turkey, and building schools in Sri Lanka.

Programs and Events

Happy Science faith centers offer regular events, programs, and seminars. Join our meditation sessions, video lectures, study groups, seminars, and book events.

Our programs will help you:

- Deepen your understanding of the purpose and meaning of life
- Improve your relationships as you learn how to love unconditionally
- Learn how to calm your mind even on stressful days through the practice of contemplation and meditation
- Learn how to overcome life's challenges

…and much more.

International Seminars

Each year, friends from all over the world join our international seminars, held at our faith centers in Japan. Different programs are offered each year and cover a wide variety of topics, including improving relationships, practicing the Eightfold Path to enlightenment, and loving yourself, to name just a few.

Happy Science Monthly

Read Master Okawa's latest lectures in our monthly booklet, Happy Science Monthly. You'll also find stories of members' life-changing experiences, news from Happy Science members around the world, in-depth information about Happy Science movies, book reviews, and much more. Happy Science Monthly is available in English, Portuguese, Spanish, French, German, Chinese, Korean, and other languages. Back issues are available upon request. Subscribe by contacting the Happy Science location nearest you.

Contact Information

Happy Science is a worldwide organization with faith centers around the globe. For a comprehensive list of centers, visit the worldwide directory at http://www.happy-science.org or www.happyscience-usa.org.

The following are some of the many Happy Science locations:

United States and Canada

New York

79 Franklin Street,
New York, NY 10013
Phone: 212-343-7972
Fax: 212-343-7973
Email: ny@happy-science.org
Website: www.happyscience-ny.org

Los Angeles

1590 E. Del Mar Boulevard,
Pasadena, CA 91106
Phone: 626-395-7775
Fax: 626-395-7776
Email: la@happy-science.org
Website: www.happyscience-la.org

San Diego

Email: sandiego@happy-science.org

San Francisco

525 Clinton Street,
Redwood City, CA 94062
Phone/Fax: 650-363-2777
Email: sf@happy-science.org
Website: www.happyscience-sf.org

Florida

12208 N 56th St.,
Temple Terrace, FL 33617
Phone:813-914-7771
Fax: 813-914-7710
Email: florida@happy-science.org
Website: www.happyscience-fl.org/

New Jersey

725 River Road, Suite 58,
Edgewater, NJ 07025
Phone: 201-313-0127
Fax: 201-313-0120
Email: nj@happy-science.org
Website: www.happyscience-usa.org

Chicago

966 Estes Ct,
Schaumburg, IL 60193
Phone/Fax: 630-284-9784
Email: chicago@happy-science.org
Website: www.happyscience-usa.org

Atlanta

1893 Piedmont Road
Atlanta, GA 30324
Phone/Fax: 404-963-6781
Email: atlanta@happy-science.org
Website: www.happyscience-atlanta.org

Hawaii

1221 Kapiolani Blvd, Suite 920,
Honolulu, HI 96814
Phone: 808-591-9772
Fax: 808-591-9776
Email: hi@happy-science.org
Website: www.happyscience-hi.org

Kauai

4504 Kukui St.,
Dragon Building Suite 21
Kapaa, HI 96746
Phone: 808-822-7007
Fax: 808-822-6007
Email: kauai-hi@happy-science.org
Website: www.happyscience-kauai.org

Toronto

323 College St.
Toronto ON M5T 1S2, Canada
Phone/Fax: 1-416-901-3747
Email: toronto@happy-science.org
Website: www.happy-science.ca

Vancouver

#212-2609 East 49th Avenue,
Vancouver, V5S 1J9, Canada
Phone: 1-604-437-7735
Fax: 1-604-437-7764
Email: vancouver@happy-science.org
Website: www.happy-science.ca

International

Tokyo

1-6-7 Togoshi, Shinagawa,
Tokyo, 142-0041 Japan
Phone: 81-3-6384-5770
Fax: 81-3-6384-5776
Email: tokyo@happy-science.org
Website: www.happy-science.org

London

3 Margaret Street,
London, W1W 8RE, UK
Phone: 44-20-7323-9255
Fax: 44-20-7323-9344
Email: eu@happy-science.org
Website: www.happyscience-uk.org

Sydney
516 Pacific Hwy Lane Cove
North,
2066 NSW Australia
Phone: 61-2-9411-2877
Fax: 61-2-9411-2822
Email: aus@happy-science.org
Website: www.happyscience.org.au

Brazil Headquarters
R. Domingos de Morais 1154,
Vila Mariana, Sao Paulo, CEP
04009-002, Brazil
Phone: 55-11-5088-3800
Fax: 55-11-5088-3806
Email: sp@happy-science.org
Website: www.happyscience-br.org

Seoul
162-17 Sadang3-dong,
Dongjak-gu, Seoul, Korea
Phone: 82-2-3478-8777
Fax: 82-2-3478-9777
Email: korea@happy-science.org
Website: www.happyscience.co.kr

Taipei
No.89, Lane 155,
Dunhua N. Rd.,
Songshan District,
Taipei City 105, Taiwan
Phone: 886-2-2719-9377
Fax: 886-2-2719-5570
Email: taiwan@happy-science.org
Website: www.irhhtw.org

Uganda
Plot 877 Rubaga Road, Kampala,
P.O. Box 34130, Kampala,
Uganda
Phone: 256-78-4728-601
Email:uganda@happy-science.org
Website: www.happyscience-uganda.org

About IRH Press

IRH Press Co., Ltd, based in Tokyo, was founded in 1987 as a publishing division of Happy Science. IRH Press publishes religious and spiritual books, journals, magazines and also operates broadcast and film production enterprises. For more information, visit OkawaBooks.com.

Other Books by Ryuho Okawa

The Nine Dimensions:
Unveiling the Laws of Eternity

The Moment of Truth:
Become a Living Angel Today

Change Your Life, Change the World:
A Spiritual Guide to Living Now

The Science of Happiness:
10 Principles for Manifesting Your Divine Nature

The Laws of the Sun:
Discover the Origin of Your Soul

The Golden Laws:
History through the Eyes of the Eternal Buddha

The Starting Point of Happiness:
A Practical and Intuitive Guide to Discovering Love, Wisdom, and Faith

Love, Nurture, and Forgive:
A Handbook to Add a New Richness to Your Life

An Unshakable Mind:
How to Overcome Life's Difficulties

The Origin of Love:
On the Beauty of Compassion

Invincible Thinking:
There is No Such Thing as Defeat

Guideposts to Happiness:
Prescriptions for a Wonderful Life

The Laws of Happiness:
The Four Principles for a Successful Life

Tips to Find Happiness:
Creating a Harmonious Home for Your Spouse, Your Children, and Yourself

The Philosophy of Progress:
Higher Thinking for Developing Infinite Prosperity

The Essence of Buddha:
The Path to Enlightenment

The Challenge of the Mind:
A Practical Approach to the Essential Buddhist Teaching of Karma

The Challenge of Enlightenment:
Realize Your Inner Potential

The Next Great Awakening:
A Spiritual Renaissance

The contents of this book were compiled from the following lectures:

Prologue: Unearthing the Universe inside Your Mind
[Kokoro no Naka no Uchū]
May 21, 1998 at Utsunomiya Buppōkan in Tochigi, Japan

Chapter 1: Becoming a World Religion
~A Paradigm Shift for Earth People~
[Sekai Shūkyō Nyūmon: Chikyūjin e no Paradaimu Shifuto]
December 4, 2010 at Yokohama Arena in Kanagawa, Japan

Chapter 2: Faith Will Bring You Miracles
[Reikai to Kiseki]
April 17, 2011 at Kokura Temple in Fukuoka, Japan

Chapter 3: A New Era of Spirituality
[Reisei no Jidai e]
July 13, 2011 at the General Headquarters in Tokyo, Japan

Chapter 4: The Arrival of the New Space Age
[Uchū Jidai e no Mezame]
August 6, 2011 at the General Headquarters in Tokyo, Japan

Chapter 5: The Time for Salvation Is Here
[Kyūsei no Toki wa Ima]
July 10, 2011 at Makuhari Messe in Chiba, Japan

https://www.happyscience-usa.org

Happy Science
USA Website

https://www.happyscience-usa.org